AF552732

SUPERVISION IN THE HOTEL INDUSTRY

SUPERVISION IN THE HOTEL INDUSTRY

By
William Lever

DISCOVERY PUBLISHING HOUSE PVT. LTD.
NEW DELHI-110 002

Published by:
Tilak Wasan

DISCOVERY PUBLISHING HOUSE PVT. LTD.
4831/24, Prahlad Street, Ansari Road
Darya Ganj, New Delhi-110002 (India)
Phone : +91-11-23279245, 43764432
Fax : +91-11-23253475
E-mail : parul.wasan@gmail.com
discoverypublishinghouse@gmail.com
info@discoverypublishinggroup.com
web : www.discoverypublishinggroup.com

***First Edition:* 2011**
ISBN: 978-81-8356-935-4

Supervision in the Hotel Industry

Printed at:
Mehra Offset Press
Delhi

PREFACE

A hotel manager or hotelier is a person who holds a management occupation within a hotel, motel, or resort establishment. Management titles and duties vary by company. In some hotels the title hotel manager or hotelier may solely be referred to the General Manager of the hotel. Small hotels may have a small management team consisting of only two or three managers while larger hotels may often have a large management team consisting of various departments and divisions. Hotel managers are generally exposed to long shifts that include late hours, weekends, and holidays due to the 24 hour operation of a hotel. The common workplace in hotels is a fast-paced environment, with high levels of interaction with guests, employees, investors, and other managers.

The caterer will probably appear around late morning time for an evening affair in order to begin the preparation work. Depending on the size and complexity of the affair, additional *mashgichim* may join those who have been working on the *kashering*. By that time, most of the utensils will likely have been *kashered* and all the worktables will have been covered with double layers of heavy duty aluminum foil and kraft paper when the table surfaces cannot be koshered. The food for the affair has been prepared offsite under kosher supervision at the caterer's commissary. As a general rule, many kashrus agencies will not permit vegetables to be checked at the site of the event, but they are checked at the commissary by the *mashgiach*. It is much too time consuming to check vegetables at the party itself.

Supervisor has got an important role to play in hotelmanagement. Supervision means overseeing the subordinates at hotel work. The supervisor is a part of the management team and he holds the designation of first line managers. He is a person who has to perform many functions which helps in achieving productivity. Therefore, supervisor can be called as the only manager who has an important role at execution level. There are certain philosophers who call supervisors as workers. There are yet some more philosophers who call them as managers. But actually he should be called as a manager or operative manager. His primary job is to manage the workers at operative level of management.This well written book will help aspiring hospitality supervisors hit the ground running with the skills they will learn in this book. They will be eqipped to juggle with expectations of management, guests, employees, and governmental agencies.

—Author

Contents

1

STAFFING AND SUPERVISION

Managing a hotel company is a task that entails broad knowledge about a lot of factors pertaining to victorious methods of achieving mammoth goals. Objectives complex in determining accomplishment derived from company supervision contain preservation of assets in the form of finances, human reserved supply and cost-effective marketing strategies. Regardless of the kind of commerce focused on, the responsibilities required in running a booming company remain similar in definition. Normal administrative skills have to be practiced firmly in order to gain trust and respect from subordinates. In this case however, tackling on hotels is a greater matter since the manager will be dealing not only with inside personnel but also outsiders, most especially minded clientele.

The role of a hotel supervisor is to coordinate and supervise the activities of hotel service workers. Their main responsibility is to maintain effective communication between the different department managers and service workers, and if done effectively will work for the common goal of generating revenue throughout the hotel.

Duties of a hotel supervisor include: maintaining a certain appearance required by the hotel dress code, know departmental procedures, policies, equipment and be prepared to explain and train co-workers in your department. Hotel Supervisors also need to promote a helpful and courteous atmosphere to guests and co-workers. At the end of the day report important information to the general manager. Have a general interest of working with people in the hotel industry.

As the boss, one has to be just and wary in completely choosing the exquisite habitancy for specifically diverse tasks. Manufacture sure that educated habitancy are watchfully recruited from the right places is critical in primarily narrowing down the hunt for good employees which are evidently hard to find these days. Once the tedious quest ends up with quality workers who in time have proven themselves more than capable of assigned duties, retention them steadily motivated comes helpful so that they stay loyal and remain active in the job. This is commonly carried out by retention laborer recognition programs or by giving out performance-based incentives.

For hotels working in a competitive environment with high quality standards cannot do without a network of advanced technological products.

Hotel Supervisor is the final result of lengthy project for the creation of a centralized real-time **supervisory** and **control system** for **all plant in the hotel** facility. Hotel Supervisor is a distributed intelligence system specifically designed for hotels or communities. The investment is amortized quickly and upgrades services within the hotel.

The user can **save energy** simply and efficiently (up to 30% on air conditioning and 20% on heating, 15% on electricity), **with the safe control of alarms**, accesses and with maximum comfort in guest rooms and other hotel areas.

One of the supervisor's responsibilities is to support the goals and requirements of upper management (the division officer and the department head). This support may take many forms, such as providing unscheduled corrective maintenance, technical reports, additional manpower for important command functions, operational training in specialized areas, or any one of a dozen other tasks that may be required of your personnel.

On occasion, you may be called upon to solve a difficult problem. If after much brainstorming, you are unable to solve the problem, you should seek assistance from the next senior person in the chain of command. Keeping a problem to yourself when you have run out of ideas will not solve it. Inform your division leading chief petty officer (LCPO) or your division officer of your problem; one of them should be able to assist you.

TRAITS OF A GOOD SUPERVISOR

Good supervisors usually have certain desirable traits. These traits are loyalty, positive thinking, genuine interest in people, initiative, decisiveness, tact and courtesy, fairness, sincerity and integrity, teaching ability, and self-confidence.

Loyalty

One trait that should stand out in every supervisor is loyalty. You must show loyalty to your country, the Navy, your unit, your superiors, and the personnel who work for you. To receive and keep the respect and loyalty of your personnel, you must be loyal yourself.

Positive Thinking

Good leaders will always be positive thinkers. They think in terms of *how* things *can* be done, not *why* they can *not* be done. They maintain an open mind to changes, new ideas, and training opportunities, Positive thinkers look to the future with confidence, and their confidence is contagious. They are enthusiastic about their jobs and the part they play in the Navy. If you want to lead others, start practicing the art of positive thinking today.

Genuine Interest in People

Did you ever meet a really great leader? If so, you probably found that instead of being cold and aloof, the person was a warm, friendly human being who seemed to make you feel important by paying close attention to what you had to say. One of the first steps you, as a supervisor, should take is to get to know your technicians personally. This not only creates a feeling that you are genuinely interested in them, but it also helps you place the right person in the right job at the right time.

You will appreciate the importance of knowing your technicians personally when the need arises for them to convert from technicians to professional defensive tacticians and fighters. Here, the wrong person in the wrong place could prove disastrous. However, you must avoid falling into the familiarity trap. Many experienced supervisors will tell you of cases where they were overly friendly with certain personnel. Then, when the time came for discipline or other adverse action, it was very difficult to deal with those personnel.

Initiative

Personnel with initiative are always needed in the naval service. Initiative is evidence of an open and alert mind. Personnel with initiative continually look for bet- ter ways to do things; they don't wait for someone else to take action.

PRACTICAL MARKETING STRATEGIES

Efficient and practical marketing strategies are known to increase added income. In this case, consistently surprising advertising schemes must be considered. For starters, brochures, tarpaulins and newspaper ads might work well as an endorsement plan. For victorious hotels frequented by preeminent habitancy worldwide, it is nevertheless critical to continue promoting the company to constantly amplify revenues. Telling the vast majority that a luxurious and elegant **hotel** exists in a single locality is made easy if a prestige for being excellent in providing a welcoming and hospitable service is built. This fact leads to other factor to be laid out in supervision which concerns accommodations.

Basic Responsibilities in Hotel Supervision

One thing that most vacationers seek when travelling is a place that offers security and security. Thus, managers of reputable hotels have to see to it that both basic needs are catered to. Providing security deposit boxes for all clients will really capture the concentration of foreigners, as not all lodges are able to gift this uncomplicated must-have. Moreover, contemplation on what guests might look for inside a room is supportive in arranging fully functional and elegant suites.

HOTEL MANAGER

A hotel manager or hotelier is a person who holds a management occupation within a hotel, motel, or resort establishment. Management titles and duties vary by company. In some hotels the title hotel manager or hotelier may solely be referred to the General Manager of the hotel. Small hotels may have a small management team consisting of only two or three managers while larger hotels may often have a large management team consisting of various departments and divisions.

A typical organizational chart for a mid-scale to large hotel:

- General Manager
  - Director of Room Operations
    - Front Office Manager
    - Front Desk Manager (s)
    - PBX Supervisor
    - Reservations Manager (may report to Sales in some hotels)
    - Guest Services Manager
    - Bell Captain
    - Concierge Supervisor
    - Executive Housekeeper
    - Housekeeping Manager(s)

  - ♦ Laundry Supervisor
  - ♦ Custodial Supervisor
- o Director of Sales & Marketing
  - ♦ Senior Sales Manager
  - ♦ Sales Manager(s)
  - ♦ Sales Coordinator (s)
  - ♦ Catering Manager
  - ♦ Marketing Manager
  - ♦ Revenue Manager
  - ♦ Convention Services Manager(s)
  - ♦ Event Manager (s)
- o Director of Food & Beverage
  - ♦ Restaurant Manager(s)
  - ♦ Room Service Manager
  - ♦ Bar Manager
  - ♦ Director of Catering
- o Chief Engineer
- o Director of Human Resources
- o Director of Security
- o Spa & Recreation Manager
- o Director of Finances / Controller
- o Director of Information Technology

Typical Qualifications For a Hotel Manager

Background and training required varies by management title and duties involved. Industry experience has proven to be an essential qualification for nearly any management occupation within the lodging industry.

Basic qualifications for a management occupation within a hotel usually consist of the following:

- Industry Experience is the main factor

- Education
  - o A high school diploma is a required qualification for any management occupation.
  - o A degree in Hospitality management studies or equivalent Business degree is often required or strongly preffered
  - o A graduate degree may be desired for a General Manager position but is often not required with sufficient management experience and tenure.

Working Conditions

Hotel managers are generally exposed to long shifts that include late hours, weekends, and holidays due to the 24 hour operation of a hotel. The common workplace in hotels is a fast-paced environment, with high levels of interaction with guests, employees, investors, and other managers.

Upper management consisting of senior managers, department heads, and General Managers may sometimes enjoy a more desirable work schedule consisting of a more traditional business day including weekdays and days off on holidays.The occupation of a hotel manager has appeared in many Hollywood films including the film Hotel Rwanda and other media outlets.

SUPERVISION AT KOSHER HOTELS

Over the past few years there has been an increase in the number of functions catered at non kosher hotels. Catering in these facilities creates many more kashrus concerns for the kosher certifying agencies supervising them. Sometimes, as many as three or four vigilant, professional *mashgichim* are needed to ensure that no requirement of kashrus is being overlooked. Whatever the number may be, there is much more involved than meets the eye. The guest enjoying a luxurious smorgasbord at these affairs really has little idea of the kashrus supervision involved. The following are some of the behind-the-scenes preparations that go into making sure that not only is the presentation of the food impeccable but the kashrus is as well.

Kashering and Set-Up By 6:00 or 7:00 a.m. on the day of the event a kashrus agency will have already sent in one or two *mashgichim* to begin preparing for the kashering. While the kosher caterer will typically send his own kosher china (or china that he rents from a kosher certified facility), there are numerous pieces of silverware and chafing dishes (A metal dish or pan mounted above a heating device used to cook food or keep it warm) and other equipment provided by the hotel that will need to be koshered. An affair calling for 500 people might require *kashering* of the following:

Reception Forks: 2000 Dinner Forks: 600 Salad Forks: 1200

Teaspoons 600 Soup Spoons: 500 Dinner Knives: 600

B&B Knives 550 Coffee Pots: 50 Serving Utensils 75

Goosenecks 100 Soup Tureens: 50 Chafing Dishes 25

Some kashrus organizations require everything to be *aino ben yomo* (more than 24 hours since its previous) before *kashering*. In such cases, a *mashgiach* must be sent to the hotel a day or two ahead of time to seal up equipment to ensure that this requirement is met. Other kashrus organizations allow for *kashering* to be done when the utensils are a *ben yomo,* or less than 24 hours old, if koshering is done with a *davar hapogem,* or caustic. In either case, the mashgiach must check that the equipment is spotlessly cleaned in order to prepare for the *kashering*. This in itself can be a long procedure and the *mashgiach* is the one to say that the equipment is ready to be koshered.

Kashering of ovens and sinks must be done in addition to the huge quantity of utensils. Depending on what is being *kashered,* either *hagala* (boiling water) or *libun* (fire or dry heat) is done. The *mashgichim* that use various cleaning fluids and boiling water for *kashering* require special skills. They must be aware of the dangers involved and take the correct precautions. In some locals, *mashgichim* must be licensed to use certain *kashering* equipment.

Hagala may take place in a piece of equipment known as steam kettle, brazier or tilt skillet. Fireman's gloves will be used to prevent accidental burning. *Kashering* can be a long procedure, depending on how many guests will be at the affair and what is being koshered.

In some contexts, there may be a separate kosher kitchen present. However, that doesn't necessary solve all the problems, because even these kitchens are, or can be, *kashered* by kashrus agencies where there was a possibility of different standard met than those of the current kashrus agency. Other hotels have only one kitchen, and it is dedicated to preparation of *treif* food. In either situation, one must bear in mind that a non-kosher hotel will often have non-kosher going on at the same time in the same kitchen as the kosher affair. Obviously this presents more of a challenge in the monitoring of the kosher affair. Non-kosher utensils typically cannot be completely removed from the kitchen and the *mashgiach* or *mashgichim* must be acutely conscious of possible mix-ups with these utensils. .

The caterer will probably appear around late morning time for an evening affair in order to begin the preparation work. Depending on the size and complexity of the affair, additional *mashgichim* may join those who have been working on the *kashering*. By that time, most of the utensils will likely have been *kashered* and all the worktables will have been covered with double layers of heavy duty aluminum foil and kraft paper when the table surfaces cannot be koshered. The food for the affair has been prepared offsite under kosher supervision at the caterer's commissary. As a general rule, many kashrus agencies will not permit vegetables to be checked at the site of the event, but they are checked at the commissary by the *mashgiach*. It is much too time consuming to check vegetables at the party itself.

All the food must be properly sealed according to *halacha*. When the food arrives at the hotel, the *mashgiach* will check that these containers are sealed and have the appropriate *simanim*. The food must then be put into the refrigerator until it will be warmed. It is very rare for a hotel to be able to designate a refrigerator just for kosher, so here too extra care must be taken. Once the prep work starts, one *mashgiach* will station himself in front of the kosher area to watch everything going on, while keeping an with eye on the *non-kosher* area, to make sure that no nonkosher food or equipment comes anywhere close to the kosher area. Another *mashgiach* will finish up any koshering that may need to be addressed and work with the caterer or the caterer's chef to review any kosher issues. For example, he may have to point out exactly which ovens and sinks can be used. Also, he will be reminded do check before doing anything that could possibly be problematic, such as removing from the general storeroom items that may not have been sent from the caterer's commissary.

Let's remember now that there must be a *mashgiach* stationed every minute at the work area because, invariably, non kosher is going on simultaneously. At about 3:00 pm, the staff, which consists of waiters, bus boys, and bartenders, arrives. Instructions must be provided to the various members of the staff regarding the affair. If they speak English, it's a little easier for the *mashgiach* to provide them instructions. If not...well, it just makes the job that much more difficult. Very often the hotel's staff are union representatives and it becomes apparent that things need to be made as easy as possible for them to only use kosher equipment.

What are some of the instructions provided to the bus boys? In a non-kosher affair, china, once used, is normally returned to the hotel's *treif* dishwasher. At a kosher affair there are designated boxes for the return of dishes supplied by the kosher caterer. Explicit instructions must be provided to the bus boys to avoid mix-ups. Waiters must also receive explicit instructions regarding many issues including from where they can take utensils, silverware and china.

Once the *kashering* is completed and the *mashgiach* has gone over instructions with the waiters, it becomes time to check the bar for the wines, whiskies and drink mixes. The knives used to cut lemons and limes and the small cutting board must be removed. All cutting of these foods must be done in the kitchen, under supervision of a *mashgiach*. The *mashgiach* must also make sure that all the bottles of approved wines, liquors, and drink mixes are contained in sealed bottles. Once the party starts, the *mashgiach* must constantly check the bar: when the bartenders run out of something, they will go back into the storeroom and many times refill a non kosher item into the empty glass flasks that were originally approved for use. If the *mashgiach* is not aware of this practice, he will never know that what he thinks is kosher wine is actually not-kosher. To try to circumvent this problem, many *mashgichim* will only allow the hotels to pour the juices and drink mixes and wines out of the original bottles to ensure what the item is. But that requirement doesn't relieve the *mashgiach* of continued vigilance. Bartenders have been known to try to take the empty kosher bottle and refill it with non kosher wines in the storeroom.

The Smorgasbord

The next area of concern is the smorgasbord. While everything might look fine and dandy, there are a number of areas of concern. First, any fish dish should be put separately from any meat dish and, if possible, a sign should alert the guests that it is a fish dish. The waiters must be instructed to put the fish item in a separate dish and not to put the fish on a plate with other food, even if the guest requests it.

Second, there are many items at the smorgasbord such as crepes and blintzes and sometimes eggs which are cooked from scratch, and which create potential *bishul akum* issues. It is necessary, in such cases, for the *mashgiach* to turn on the burners. Unfortunately, the fires on these burners are constantly going out, many times due to either the air conditioning in the hall or a malfunctioning burner, or other problems. Thus the *mashgiach* must always be circulating around the smorgasbord.

During and After the Affair

So far, we have *mashgichim* who have been on their feet approximately 12 hours and are not nearly through. Special care must be taken that during serving of the main course, only the caterer's kosher utensils or whatever was koshered may only be used. Very often a *mashgiach* will be stationed by the non-kosher silverware to redirect the waiters during set up. Waiters must be constantly watched as they go in and out of the kitchen to be sure they are not grabbing the wrong utensils.

An additional area of concern is the nondairy creamer served at dessert. Any food returning to the commissary has been, or should have been, properly sealed by the *mashgiach*. One of the concerns when dessert rolls around is that it is very easy for the waiters to grab milk which, many times, is located outside of the kitchen near the coffee urns and bring the milk out to be served at dessert or the Viennese table. The only way to monitor that is for all caterers to serve portion control servings of nondairy creamer as opposed to little metal creamers that are filled up with milk and put out on the tables.

By this time the *mashgichim* have been on their feet for about 16 hours and are ready to leave. They must however take steps to ensure that only the caterer's *keylim* are sent back to the commissary and not the hotel utensils.

We have taken only a small look at the behind the scenes preparations to ensure that everything was done according to exacting and demanding kashrus standards that guests would, and should, expect. A guest should never be hesitant to question the *mashgiach* at an affair, before he starts eating, as to what the standards of the kashrus organization are and if the *mashgiach* did everything necessary for the guest to be completely satisfied with the kashrus standards for that event.

HOSPITALITY MANAGEMENT STUDIES

Hospitality management studies provides a focus on management of hospitality operations including hotels, restaurants, cruise ships, amusement parks, destination marketing organizations, convention centers, country clubs, and related industries.

It is the academic study of the hospitality industry. A degree in Hospitality management is often conferred from either a university college dedicated to the studies of hospitality management or a business school with a department in hospitality management studies. Degrees in hospitality management may also be referred to as hotel management, hotel and tourism management, or hotel administration. Degrees conferred in this academic field include Bachelors of Arts, Bachelors of Business Administration, Bachelors of Science, Masters of Science, MBA, and Doctorate of Philosophy.

In America, Hospitality and Tourism Management curriculum follow similar core subject applications to that of a business degree but with a focus on hospitality management. Core subject areas include accounting, administration, finance, information systems, marketing, human resource management, public relations, strategy, quantitative methods, and sectoral studies in the various areas of hospitality business.

Cornell University, University of Nevada, Las Vegas (UNLV), and University of Central Florida (UCF) are considered the top Hospitality Management undergraduate colleges in America. One of the newest graduate degree programs in hospitality management is offered by The George Washington University School of Business in Washington, D.C..

In addition to the core coursework above, degree-specific coursework normally includes:

- Restaurant Management (Examples: Management of Food and Beverage Operations, Food Science, Food Selection and Preparation, Food and Beverage Cost Control)
- Lodging Operations (Examples: Lodging Management, Hotel Operations, Resort Timeshare Management, Reservation Sales and Marketing, Hospitality Physical Plant)
- Global Tourism (Examples: Tourism Management, Airline Industry, Sustainable Tourism, Hospitality and Research Methods)
- Attractions Management (Examples: Theme Park Management, Entertainment Arts)

- Event Management (Examples: Event Industry, Catering Management, Hospitality Marketing Management)
- Food Preparation (Examples: Basic Food Preparation, Food Sanitation, Beer and Wine Labs)

Many hospitality programs require concurrent field experience within the industry in the form of internships or cooperative placements.

Graduate Placement

Several large hospitality corporations such as Marriott, Hilton Worldwide, IHG, Hyatt, Sasi park, Wyndham, beeran international Parks and Resorts, and various management companies offer internship programs as well as management training programs and direct placements for students majoring in Hospitality and Tourism Management. Similar to other business fields, management training programs and direct placement opportunities are highly competitive.

Hospitality Management in The Netherlands

Tio University (in Utrecht) provides the Hotel and Event management study in English and Dutch.

Hospitality Management in The Stellenbosch South Africa

The management techniques and practices of the hospitality industry in the United States are viewed as the best in the world. AHA South Africa's academic programmess are designed to meet the growing needs of the hospitality industry by placing equal emphasis on attitude and aptitude. Students graduate with AHA's IHMS' world-class Diploma in International Hospitality Management (DIHM).

The aim of the DIHM Programme is to offer students, who wish to begin working at the supervisory level within the industry, a comprehensive hospitality management education. Students will be introduced to all aspects of hospitality services operations, and the wide array of career opportunities available within the industry.

Upon successful completion of the DIHM Programme, it is expected that graduates will have developed:

1. The technical and supervisory management skills and product knowledge necessary for a career in the hospitality industry.
2. The ability to think logically and communicate clearly.
3. An inter-disciplinary approach to problem-solving and decision-making.
4. A global perspective on the operations of the industry.

Course Curriculum

Semester One Code Title HM 101 Introduction to Hospitality and Tourism SOC 101 Service Basics SOC 102 Cultural Diversity COM 101 Language of Hospitality COM 102 Computer Applications FB 101 Food and Beverage Service CA 101 Introduction to Culinary Arts CA 102 Health and Food Safety FB 103 Cape Wine Academy Prelim Course WBL Work Based Learning (30 Hours)

Semester Two Code Title COM 103 Business Communication FB 102 Revenue and Menu Management FB104 Food and Beverage Management FB 105 Wines of the World HM 103 Event Planning HM 104 Inventory and Purchasing HM105 Hospitality Accounting CA 103 Quantity Food Production CA 104 Nutrition WBL Work Based Learning (30 hours)

Semester Three Code Title COM 105 Business Entrepreneurship SOC 103 Leadership Development HM 106 Front Office Operations HM 107 Lodging Management HM 108 Sales and Marketing HM 109 Human Resource Management WBL Work Based Learning (120 hours)

Grading System

We understand that students learn in many different ways and we do our best to broaden the means by which we assess them accordingly. Students will be assessed on class participation in discussions, assignments, discussion of articles, and practical applications with components of each complete module and other activities as well as through the more traditional means of quizzes and examinations.

Attendance is important and is a part of the final assessment. Participation is also highly valued, as we strive to produce graduates who have a good work ethic, strive for excellence, are willing to go the extra mile in their future careers and come to work with a positive, willing-to-do-whatever-it-takes approach. We therefore reward the development of those values in class participation.

Grading Scale

Performance of students will be rated at the end of each semester in accordance with the following grading system. Grade Denotes Percent Range % A+ = Outstanding 96 - 100 A = Excellent 91 - 95 B+ = Very Good 86 - 90 B = Good 81 - 85 C+ = Satisfactory 76 - 80 C = Pass 70 - 75 F = Fail 0 - 69 INC = Incomplete

We apply continuous assessment at the Private Hotel School. Students are therefore assessed on their performance during the semester as well as an examination at the end of the semester.

Passing Grade

Students must receive a grade of "C" (minimum 70%) to pass in each subject. A student, who incurs a grade of "F" in any course, is required to retake the course and obtain a passing grade. Any financial implications of retaking a course will be at a cost of R4600.

Attendance

The PHS aims to prepare students to be successful professionals. Attendance and punctuality are important work ethics for students to develop. An attendance of at least 80% in all theoretical classes and 90% of all practical classes is required.

The total of excused absences should therefore not exceed 20% of theoretical course hours and 10% of practical course hours. Students who are absent, whether excused or unexcused, in more than the indicated requirements, are considered to have officially withdrawn from that course and will be given a grade of "F" in that course.

HOSPITALITY SERVICE

The concept of hospitality exchange, also known as "accommodation sharing", "hospitality services", and "home stay networks", refers to centrally organized social networks of individuals, generally travelers, who offer or seek accommodation without monetary exchange. These services generally connect users via the internet.

In 1949, Bob Luitweiler founded the first hospitality service called Servas Open Doors as a cross national, non-profit, volunteer run organization advocating interracial and international peace. In 1965, John Wilcock set up the Traveler's Directory as a listing of his friends willing to host each other when traveling.

In 1988, Joy Lily rescued the organization from imminent shutdown, forming Hospitality Exchange. In 1970 Jimmy Carter (then US President) announced the formation of Friendship Force International which has chapters in 57 countries today. In 2000, Veit Kuhne founded Hospitality Club, the first Internet-based service. In 2004, Casey Fenton started CouchSurfing, now the largest hospitality exchange organization.

How They Work

Generally, after registering, members have the option of providing very detailed information and pictures of themselves and of the sleeping accommodation being offered, if any. The more information provided by a member improves the chances that someone will find the member trustworthy enough to be their host or guest. Names and addresses may be verified by volunteers. Members looking for accommodation can search for hosts using several parameters such as age, location, sex, and activity level.

Home stays are entirely consensual between the host and guest, and the duration, nature, and terms of the guest's stay are generally worked out in advance to the convenience of both parties. No monetary exchange takes place except under certain circumstances (e.g. the guest may compensate the host for food). After using the service, members can leave a noticeable reference about their host or guest.

Instead of or in addition to accommodation, members also offer to provide guide services or travel-related advice. The websites of the networks also provide editable travel guides and forums where members may seek travel partners or advice. Many such organizations are also focused on "social networking" and members organize activities such as camping trips, bar crawls, meetings, and sporting events.

Some networks cater to specific niche markets such as students, activists, religious pilgrims, and even occupational groups like police officers.

Benefits

As these networks provide accommodation at no charge, monetary savings can be significant. Hospitality exchange gives travelers the chance to experience what life is like for people living in other places. In addition, making interpersonal connections and fostering understanding of different cultures may in the long run also be important to international relations.

During hospitality exchanges, hosts may show off their local knowledge and exciting places "off the tourist map". Not only may travelers get a distinct experience, but they will also get a feel for the everyday lives of local residents.

Reciprocity

The concept behind Hospitality services is based on the pay it forward philosophy, gift economy, and reciprocal altruism.

Drawbacks

Lack of Guarantee

There is no contractual agreement between users in these systems. Reservations are made, but if they are for some reason broken, there is no higher authority to which one could plead for a refund or other compensation. The only repercussion will be the poor rating you give that user and your only consolation will be that your warning will deter others from visiting or hosting them. For those who feel insecure unless their travel arrangements are written in stone before departure, this system will not be comforting.

Potential Interpersonal Conflict or Awkwardness

There is a chance that guest and host will not get along. Perhaps there will be scheduling or ideological conflicts. Maybe you will find that hosts or visitors have misrepresented themselves. Perhaps the experience will not live up to your expectations. Intense interpersonal communications in advance and a flexibility once you have arrived is your best bet.

These experiences require additional planning and courtesy towards the demands of your host. Thus, your living conditions, length of stay, and overall experience will be circumscribed by the living conditions you enter into.

Digital Divide and Demographic Segregation

As use of these services generally requires access to the internet and knowledge of the English language, the sample population found in searches of these databases is really much less diverse than a geographical representation of worldwide users might suggest.

Security

Staying in someone's house, or inviting people into your house leaves open the possibility of being taken advantage of.

Example Networks

There are countless websites that serve the idea of hospitality service, with new ones appearing as this phenomenon becomes more popular. While this page is not intended to be a directory listing, here is a small sample of the well-established and long-standing networks:

- CouchSurfing - A very active network with over 2 million members in more than 200 countries
- Friendship Force International A network of chapters worldwide which concentrates on building understanding across cultures.
- Hospitality Club - A very active network with over 550,000 members in more than 200 countries
- Servas International - human rights and global peace oriented since 1949. A relatively small network now with over 15,000 members with a very long history.
- Tripping - A global network of travelers with the motto "For Travelers, Not Tourists"
- BeWelcome

SUPERVISOR

A supervisor, foreperson, team leader, overseer, cell coach, facilitator, or area coordinator is a manager in a position of trust in business.The US Bureau of Census has four hundred titles under the supervisor classification.

An employee is a supervisor if they have the power and authority to do the following actions (according to the Ontario Ministry of Labour):

1. Give instructions and/or orders to subordinates.
2. Be held responsible for the work and actions of other employees.

If an employee cannot do the above, legally he or she is probably not a supervisor, but in some other category, such as lead hand.

A supervisor is first and foremost an overseer whose main responsibility is to ensure that a group of subordinates get out the assigned amount of production, when they are supposed to do it and within acceptable levels of quality, costs and safety.

A Supervisor is responsible for the productivity and actions of a small group of employees. The Supervisor has several manager-like roles, responsibilities, and powers. Two of the key differences between a Supervisor and a Manager are (1) the Supervisor does not typically have "hire and fire" authority, and (2) the Supervisor does not have budget authority.

Lacking "hire and fire" authority means that a Supervisor may not recruit the employees working in the Supervisor's group nor does the Supervisor have the authority to terminate an employee. The Supervisor may participate in the hiring process as part of interviewing and assessing candidates, but the actual hiring authority rests in the hands of a Human Resource Manager. The Supervisor may recommend to management that a particular employee be terminated and the Supervisor may be the one who documents the behaviors leading to the recommendation but the actual firing authority rests in the hands of a Manager.

Lacking budget authority means that a Supervisor is provided a budget developed by management within which constraints the Supervisor is expected to provide a productive environment for the employees of the Supervisor's work group. A Supervisor will usually have the authority to make purchases within specified limits.

A Supervisor is also given the power to approve work hours and other payroll issues. Normally, budget affecting requests such as travel will require not only the Supervisor's approval but the approval of one or more layers of management.

As a member of management, a supervisor's main job is more concerned with orchestrating and controlling work rather than performing it directly.

Responsibilities

A supervisor in the workplace has four distinctly separate sets of responsibilities. The supervisor's first duty is to represent management and the company. It is the supervisor's job to organize his/her department and employees, visualize future impacts and needs, energize the employees to get their tasks done and supervise their work ensuring that the productivity and quality standards are met. To ensure that this is done, the supervisor makes certain that his employees have the training, the tools and the material that they need to carry out their duties.

Another important part of the job is to act as a middleman and buffer between the employees who perform the daily tasks and the rest of the organization who is not directly involved in day to day tasks. The supervisor makes sure that their employees' pay is correct, their vacation pay arrives on time and they receive proper care if they get injured on the job.

Training

Supervisors often do not require any formal education on how they are to perform their duties but are most often given on-the-job training or attend company sponsored courses. Many employers have supervisor handbooks that need to be followed. Supervisors must be aware of their legal responsibilities to ensure that their employees work safely and that the workplace that they are responsible for meets government standards.

Science

In science, a supervisor is a senior scientist that, along with their own responsibilities, aids and guides a postgraduate research student, or undergraduate student, in their research project; offering both moral support and scientific insight and guidance.

A supervisor of any type carries on the responsibility of "supervising" his/her workers and making sure work is getting done. It is a challenging role, yet rewarding, when a supervisor and the team has meet their goal. What makes a good supervisor? . Or better yet, what makes an over-the-top supervisor? In this article, you'll get some brief supervisor training tips recognized as the three I's.

Initiate change-When work productivity is not meeting expectations, supervisors carry on the responsibility to initiate change. For example, envision an assembly line of several workers lined up in a row, each with a certain task that will contribute to the final product. What would happen if the first person in the line did not make his/her quota or starts falling behind in with production?

As a result, the second person might not be able to contribute because his/her role is based upon the first person's duties and so on. This chain reaction of work productivity will only get worse unless a supervisor steps up to make a change. There are several possibilities to what this supervisor could do. Probation may be an easy answer for some, but with effective supervisor training, a good leader will discover a way to make things work without having to compromise any work standards.

Reorganizing the line of workers, cross-training, and confronting the individual about his/her drop in performance could provide insight, answers, and solutions that a supervisor can execute upon. Initiating change isn't just about putting someone on probationary status or switching roles and hiring someone else that will do the job. A good supervisor will strategically handle problems and find new solutions that will make the work environment continuously more productive and operate more smoothly.

Introduce new ideas-A resourceful supervisor who entices employees with new ideas in the workplace will serve as a successful problem solver and motivating role model. For example, a supervisor could observe work conditions as monotonous, unmotivated and sense that workers are getting burned out from daily work. He or she could ask themselves, 'What can I do myself to motivate my workers?' or 'How can we fix this problem at work?' Brainstorming and executing new ideas at work will help broaden the possibilities of the ideal work setting, or what works best in each situation. Supervisors providing new ideas will help keep workers active and rejuvenated and thus keep them from reaching job dissatisfaction and complacency.

Influence others-A charismatic and hard working supervisor will earn the respect of his/her employees. Not too many individuals want to work for a supervisor who doesn't practice what he/she preaches—or carries a negative aura everywhere? An influential supervisor will get involved and take a moment to help their employees out with a difficult project or task. A supervisor who influences others but also motivates workers to influence each other will foster a continuous circle of positive emotions. Workers are more inclined to work harder when they see that their supervisor is equally working his/her part.

Using these three "I's of supervisor training tips will provide you with a foundation to organize and run your group of workers more effectively, whether you are currently a supervisor, or will be transitioning to one in the future.

WAITING STAFF

A waiter or waitress ensures that guests receive prompt attention and service when they enter the restaurant.

Waiting staff, wait staff, or wait staff are those who work at a restaurant or a bar attending customers — supplying them with food and drink as requested. Traditionally, a male waiting tables is called a "waiter" and a female a "waitress" with the gender-neutral version being a "server". Other gender-neutral versions include using "*waiter*" indiscriminately for males and females, "*waitperson*", or the Americanism "*waitron*", which was coined in the 1980s.

Duties:

- set table cutlery, serviettes and condiments before the start of meals;

- seat the guests when they arrive, take their orders, and serve food and beverages;
- familiarise yourself with the menu and recommend dishes, drinks and wines when taking orders;
- clear used cutlery and replace table settings when guests leave;
- serve individual portions or dishes and refill drinks when requested.

Waiting on tables is (along with nursing and teaching) part of the service sector, and among the most common occupations in the United States. The Bureau of Labor Statistics estimates that, as of May 2008, there were over 2.2 million persons employed as servers in the U.S. Many servers are required by their employers to wear a uniform.

Personal Qualities:

- **Must be neat, tidy and smartly dressed**
- Tactful, courteous and able to communicate well with people
- A good service attitude
- Able to work in a team
- A good memory to recall which customer ordered which dish
- Must have good physical health as the waiter spends most of his working hours on his feet
- Manual dexterity required to serve guests

Taking Orders

The duties of waiting staff include preparing tables for a meal, taking customers' orders, serving drinks and food, and cleaning up before, after and during servings in a restaurant. Silver service staff are specially trained to serve at banquets or high-end restaurants. They follow specific rules of service and it is a skilled job.

They generally wear black and white with a long, white apron (extending from the waist to ankle). The head server is in charge of the waiting staff, and is also frequently responsible for assigning seating. The functions of a head server can overlap to some degree with that of the maître d'hôtel. Some restaurants employ busboys or busgirls, increasingly referred to as bussers, to clear dirty dishes, set tables, and otherwise assist the waiting staff.

Tipping

In the United States, United Kingdom, Canada, many other Western countries and parts of the Middle East, it is customary for customers to pay a tip to a server after a meal, with a possible range from 15% to 30% depending on the level and quality of service. In some situations, a tip or "service charge" will be included on the restaurant bill in the U.S. Also called a gratuity, a "service charge" will be automatically applied for situations where the restaurant management imposes this to ensure that the servers working in such situations earn their usual tip income.

Such service charges are usually around 18%; an additional voluntary tip is sometimes given. There is some debate in the U.S. whether a "minimum tip" exists as a convention; some argue that 15% or 20% is a minimum tip or that it is extremely rude to not leave at least $1, even if the service was not up to standard. However, some people also believe that a "minimum tip" is a way for employers to shift the responsibility of paying employee wages onto the customer. These issues are regional, cultural, and very subjective.

In Germany and other Western countries, where minimum wages exist for servers and where tipping is not culturally entrenched, most tips take the form of rounding up to the nearest whole or half denomination of currency when the server is cashing a party out at their table. In the United Kingdom it is common practice to tip 10% of the cost of the meal.

By contrast, servers in Japan refuse tips because it isn't a Japanese custom.

Tipping is not customary in Asia, Australia and New Zealand and is not factored into wages of staff, however tips may be appreciated. This is especially the case if the customer or party has been unusually difficult or has left a mess - parents of small children, for example, may leave a small tip. In these countries, tips are often placed into a Tip Jar and pooled rather than being kept by individual servers. This money is usually then spent on things that directly benefit staff - it may be used to maintain staff facilities or to fund events such as Christmas parties, for example.

In Taiwan and Hong Kong, a 10% service fee is often added to meals in middle-to-upscale restaurants. However, this fee does not go to the waitstaff - but is simply a surcharge that is added to the price of the meal.

Where tipping is common, it may be encouraged as a social convention, but on occasion may actually be vehemently enforced by the restaurant.

BOTTLE SERVICE

Bottle service is a feature of many upscale bars and nightclubs where patrons may purchase entire bottles of liquor for their personal consumption.The purchase of bottle service typically includes a reserved table for the patron's party and mixers of the patron's choice. Bottle service can include the service of a VIP host, who will ensure that patrons have sufficient mixers and will often make drinks using the patrons' liquor bottle and mixers. The purchase of bottle service sometimes results in cover charge being waived for the purchaser's party, and often allows patrons to bypass entrance lines.

The cost of a bottle at such a bar or club is usually extremely marked up, often by 2000% or more (20×), and can account for a significant portion of an establishment's revenue. Early forms of bottle service existed in World War II era Japan, where unfinished bottles would be stored. In its modern form, an early example was in 1988 at the Paris nightclub *Les Bains Douches,* bottle service was introduced to deal with an excess of customer demand.

An early, inexpensive form of bottle service ($90, compared with $6 drinks) was established at the *Tunnel* in 1993 (by Jeffrey Jah and Mark Baker). The modern form of bottle service was pioneered in 1995 by Michael Ault at *Spy Bar* and in 1996, *Chaos* ($175 for a bottle of Stolichnaya vodka),with the express goal of creating a "barrier to entry", rather than of increasing liquor sales. The concept later spread to other American cities, notably Miami and Las Vegas in the early 2000s.

2

Mantras for Successful Managers

World renowned hotel marketing coach Neil Salerno writes, "One of the nice things about being in the twilight of a thirty-year career in the hotel industry is that it gives one the ability to reflect back on the many great people who have shaped and influenced that career. After many years in hotel operations as well as sales and marketing, both on-property and as a corporate V.P., I was exposed to many different managers and their management styles."

Management styles, experience, and talent are as varied as their numbers, but they all had something to offer if one paid attention. Observing people and their habits has always been sort of a hobby for me. I believe that everyone has something to offer if you are looking to learn from them.

I (Neil) would like to think that I learned something from each and every one of them; even if it was only to decide which traits I did or did not want to emulate. I could probably write an entire book detailing the actions and styles of the worst of these managers, but most people don't recognize their own bad traits, even if outlined in an article, so that would be fruitless.

Recently, a client asked me what I thought the most successful general managers have in common; what makes the best managers stand head and shoulders above the others.

Circumstances certainly have great influence on ultimate success; outstanding hotels can produce successful managers. But what traits make a good manager rise above given circumstances; creating success where there was none and creating even greater success where it already existed.

The Best Hotel General Manager I ever met accepts responsibility for top-line revenue.

All too often, I have heard managers lament how they would have made more profit if only they had more top-line revenue; as if hinting that increased revenue was out of their direct control. The fact is that many general managers feel a detachment from their hotel's revenue lines. Ironically, this most often occurs when revenues are failing. Accepting ownership of poor revenues as well as healthy revenues is a telltale sign of a good general manager.

The best general manager I ever met takes responsibility for revenue production, whether or not he/she has a separate sales team. The best general manager is the true sales leader at the hotel; involved in every aspect of generating business. The best general manager leads morning sales meetings; displaying his/her personal involvement. The best managers know their top producing clients and contribute to servicing them.

For hotels lucky enough to have a sales team, the best general manager takes on specific hotel sales accounts; both, to be involved in larger accounts, and to be an example to the sales team. Sales leadership is the most important general management role.

Many articles have been written extolling the necessary skills and work habits of hotel sales people, but little is said about the role of general managers in the sales process. We have all seen how easily a poor general manager can negatively influence even the best people on their staff. By contrast, there are many mediocre people that have been guided to lofty success by great general managers.

As a corporate vice president, I always found it interesting to see whether or not a general manager got involved in sales training programs. Anyone who has done property sales training can tell you how seldom general managers participate in these programs. I don't know who decided to separate sales from operations, but the best general managers have the ability to merge these functions into powerful programs.

Sadly, many companies set themselves up for failure by directing sales activities with the sales team without the participation of the one who is truly responsible...the general manager. The best general manager I ever met would never let this happen.

During my coaching programs with various owners and general managers, I have heard many managers pound their chests with pride because they sometimes make sales calls with their sales people. This is great, but do they remain involved in the progress of those accounts? Do they demonstrate to the sales team that follow-up is the key to booking business, by their own follow-up practices? For some, it's merely a good way to get out of the building for a little while.

The best general manager I ever met reviews and signs off on all sales activity for his/her team; and directs new activity through the hotel director of sales or directly if no sales director exists. The best general manager I ever met functions as the true director of sales. Now some directors of sales might take exception to this statement, but experienced sales directors know how much easier their job can be when the G.M. is involved in the process.

The best general manager takes on the sales role, where there is no sales team, through intense community involvement, reading to find new ideas, and constantly seeking ways to improve business.

The best general manager leads the hotel's e-Marketing effort for web site, GDS, and third-party aggregators. These areas demand G.M. involvement; even if the hotel is lucky enough to have a dedicated revenue manager.

The Best Hotel General Manager I ever met is focused on success.

This trait may sound quite basic to many of you, but focus can be elusive. Focus, in this sense, is what prompts a manager to analyze each hotel profit center to target improvements in successful programs as well as failing ones. Managers who concentrate only on failing areas have a tendency to play the catch-up game, constantly putting out fires to save failing programs, while successful programs go bad from neglect. Some failing programs need to be allowed to disappear.

Focus is what directs a manager towards those activities which matter most. The best general manager realizes that just being busy is not as important as being busy doing the right things. The 80/20 rule is amazing in its myriad of applications; 20 percent of everything you do will result in 80 percent of your successes. Finding the right 20 percent takes focus.

The Best Hotel General Manager I ever met looks for small successes.

I could not count the number of times I have heard hotel team members lament about being criticized for doing wrong, yet being ignored when things go right. I can't imagine how frustrating this can be. The best general managers look for his/her team's small successes and reward them, even if it is only a public "well done". This may sound simple and basic to some of you, but it's less common than you might think.

For those of you who think you do these well, think again. Often an insincere facial expression or casual insincere comment belies the true intent a manager seeks. Praise in public, criticize in private; the best general manager I ever met looks for opportunities to provide sincere rewards. A sincere comment can be the biggest job motivator.

The Best Hotel General Manager I ever met is a great communicator.

Communicating is a two-way process; talking and listening. As I teach new sales people, having two ears and only one mouth should indicate that one should listen twice as much as talking. The best general manager I ever met demonstrates this daily.

Managers who listen to their teammates find new opportunities to help them perform their jobs better. Good leadership comes from understanding the needs of the team. Understanding comes from listening, not from smooth talk.

RESPONSES IN LONDON HOTELS

Hoteliers in London often ask me how to deal with TripAdvisor comments. A recent survey by TripAdvisor/ Market Metrix found that 85% of hotels have no guidelines on how to handle negative guest reviews published online.

To address this issue, I would like to look at London hotels that appear to do this well. I hope this will encourage others to follow suit, knowing that complaint recovery is one of the best ways to build customer loyalty.

We all love to use TripAdvisor, but it does have faults. Occasionally, people use the site malevolently.

I know one very solid London hotel where someone posted a lot of negative comments when they returned home and asked friends and family (who had of course never stayed at the hotel) to do the same. These negative comments went against the grain of most other reviews in a hotel where I personally know the management to be very diligent.

If the hotel can prove foul play in such cases, management should contact TripAdvisor directly to see if invalid comments can be removed. TripAdvisor is usually understanding and even-handed in these situations. It's not about whether a hotel gets complaints but how well – and how personally – it responds to them.

But back to the original question: assuming a negative comment is genuine, how should hotel management respond to it, if at all?

Some hotels put in standard responses – the worst possible solution.

By entering some "blah blah" about how you value their feedback, etc. (without addressing the specific underlying issue) a hotel's management is simply being arrogant. It's better not to bother responding at all.

Other hotels respond to negative comments by thanking the guest (which is a good start) and then mentioning some specific steps they have taken.

Better still, they may actually give ownership of the issue to the hotel department head responsible for that area, who responds in person.

That for me underlines that complaints are a genuine improvement opportunity – if the hotel in question is fundamentally well-run of course.

One hotel that does this well is the Lanesborough. I admire its management, the staff training, its hi-tech amenities (including free WiFi) and the ethos of transparent pricing which is so unusual in super-luxury hotels.

The Lanesborough takes a diligent, personal approach towards online guest reviews. Whenever a comment appears on TripAdvisor, the relevant department head at the Lanesborough actually follows up on the specific experience that led to the comment. The response is then personal, written by the person directly responsible and acknowledges the issue raised.

The Lanesborough is by no means a cheap hotel – in fact it houses one of London's four most expensive hotel rooms within its distinguished walls. But I'm impressed that it is not too snooty to respond to TripAdvisor reviews (when several of its top-end competitors in London do not seem to bother acknowledging online guest comments at all).

Now, let's take a look another hotel that goes even further: Threadneedles Hotel in the City, which currently has a very respectable ranking in the top 40 London hotels (and has been rising steadily up the charts).

I love the fact that the hotel's management is confident enough to admit mistakes and tries engaging with the few guests who complain. They even use phrases like "We are very sorry for the terrible service you experienced..." which is brave and gives them great credibility.

I recall a comment made to me once by the former Hilton CEO. He candidly said that in a people-driven business like hotels you're always "missing the target": it's all about rectifying the situation superbly when this occurs.

Unlike many hotels, Threadneedles Hotel addresses its few online guest complaints head-on and with humility. It's clear that management closely read the complaint, acknowledge any errors and then describe what they've done to address it. The focus on "customer recovery" after a complaint is fixed is admirable.

The vast majority of the Threadneedle's guest reviews are positive. In those cases too, the hotel's management will thank the guest and invite him or her to contact them directly if a return visit is planned.

Mr Brian Tapson, who is Assistant General Manager at the hotel, has kindly shared some of the hotel's internal standards with London Hotels Insight:

- All guest feedback is responded to on a personal level.
- Both positive and negative feedback is addressed within 24 hours.
- Guest feedback helps to continuously shape policies and training.
- All guest reviews are shared with and communicated to staff.

These are simple standards, consistently executed. I wish more hotels followed this lead: congratulations to the Threadneedles Hotel!

Here are some key skills and abilities that help anyone be a better manager.

Need For Good Managers Increasing

The need for good managers is not going away. It is intensifying. With 'flatter' organizations and self-directed teams becoming common; with personal computers and networks making information available to more people more quickly;

the raw number of managers needed is decreasing. However, the need for good managers, people who can manage themselves and others in a high stress environment, is increasing.

I believe anyone can be a good manager. It is as much trainable skill as it is inherent ability; as much science as art. Here are some things that make you a better manager:

As a Person

- You have confidence in yourself and your abilities. You are happy with who you are, but you are still learning and getting better.
- You are something of an extrovert. You don't have to be the life of the party, but you can't be a wallflower. Management is a people skill - it's not the job for someone who doesn't enjoy people.
- You are honest and straight forward. Your success depends heavily on the trust of others.
- You are an includer not an excluder. You bring others into what you do. You don't exclude other because they lack certain attributes.
- You have a 'presence'. Managers must lead. Effective leaders have a quality about them that makes people notice when they enter a room.

On the Job

- You are consistent, but not rigid; dependable, but can change your mind. You make decisions, but easily accept input from others.
- You are a little bit crazy. You think out-of-the box. You try new things and if they fail, you admit the mistake, but don't apologize for having tried.
- You are not afraid to "do the math". You make plans and schedules and work toward them.
- You are nimble and can change plans quickly, but you are not flighty.

- You see information as a tool to be used, not as power to be hoarded.

Take a look at yourself against this list. Find the places where you can improve and then get going. And , if you need help, remember that's what this site is all about - Helping new managers get started and experienced managers get better.

SALES MANAGEMENT

Sales management is attainment of an organization's sales goals in an effective & efficient manner through planning, staffing, training, leading & controlling organizational resources. Revenue, sales, and sources of funds fuel organizations and the management of that process is the most important function.

Sales Planning

An essential sales leadership role is to establish a sense of purpose or vision and clear direction to get there. A key element of a business' strategic 12-month plan is to answer the question: "Where will all the sales come from?" The sales plan is not a guesstimate. It takes its direction from the marketing strategy and is based on thorough research and a considered positioning of the company within the market place.

Sales planning involves predicting demand for the product and demand on the sales assets (machines, people, or a combination of both). Faiiure to plan always means lost sales. Planning insures that when a consumer wishes to purchase the product, the product is available, but it also means opportunities for additional sales are presented and the sales assets are available to exploit these opportunities.

Planning should allow for meeting increasing customer demand for more products, services and/or customization as the business is growing, but also react quickly when demand decreases. Sales planning improves efficiency and decreases unfocused and uncoordinated activity within the sales process.

Sales Reporting

The sales reporting includes the key performance indicators of the sales force. The key performance Indicators indicate whether or not the sales process is being operated effectively and achieves the results as set forth in sales planning. It should enable the sales managers to take timely corrective action deviate from projected values. It also allows senior management to evaluate the sales manager.

More "results related" than "process related" are information regarding the sales funnel and the hit rate. Sales reporting can provide metrics for sales management compensation. Rewarding the best managers without accurate and reliable sales reports is not objective.

Also, sales reports are made for internal use for top management. If other divisions' compensation plan depends on final results, it is needed to present results of sales department's work to other departments.

Finally, sales reports are required for investors, partners and government, so the sales management system should have advanced reporting capabilities to satisfy the needs of different stakeholders.

CHIEF EXECUTIVE OFFICER

A chief executive officer (CEO, American English), managing director (MD, British English), or chief executive is the highest-ranking corporate officer (executive) or administrator in charge of total management of an organization. An individual appointed as a CEO of a corporation, company, organization, or agency reports to the board of directors.

Many CEOs have the title "president and CEO". This is a popular combination especially if someone else is a non-executive chairman of the board. In addition, it can mean the opposite (especially in the United States), in other words that the title holders are also inside directors on the board of directors if not the chairperson (often called "president"), or it can mean that they are also the chief operating officer. Compared to the CEO, the president is often considered to be more focused upon daily operations, who is supposed to be the visionary, so the title "president and CEO" is often used to emphasise that the title holder performs both these roles.

Responsibilities

The responsibility of the chief executive officer is to align the company, internally and externally, with his or her strategic vision. The core duty of a CEO is to facilitate business outside of the company while guiding employees and other executive officers towards a central objective. The size and sector of the company will dictate the secondary responsibilities. A CEO must have a balance of internal and external initiatives to build a sustainable company.

- For corporations, the chief executive officer primarily coordinates external initiatives at a high level. As there are many other c-level executives (e.g. marketing, information, technical, financial etc.), seldom do corporate CEOs have low-level functions.
- For emerging entrepreneurs, their acting position as a CEO is much different than that on the corporate level. As often other c-level executives are not incorporated in small operations, it is the duty of the CEO (and sometimes founder) to assume those positions.
- Mid-sized companies borrow from corporate and entrepreneurial CEO responsibilities. There will not be all c-level positions available so the CEO must compensate for gaps either through delegating or assuming additional responsibility.

In many states, when an organization incorporates it is necessary to specify individuals in the role of president, treasurer, and secretary with the provison that the person nominated as president cannot also hold the position of treasurer. But often a person can be specified as secretary/ treasurer.

In many non-profits, there is a gross confusion between the chair of the board (sometimes referred to as the president of the board), the secretary of the board (also confused with the secretary of the corporation), and then a board often creates the position of treasurer. Boards should not have presidents or treasurers, but boards and corporations both need secretaries.

International Use

In some European Union countries, there are two separate boards, one executive board for the day-to-day business and one supervisory board for control purposes (elected by the shareholders). In these countries, the CEO presides over the executive board and the chairman presides over the supervisory board, and these two roles will always be held by different people. This ensures a distinction between management by the executive board and governance by the supervisory board. This allows for clear lines of authority.

The aim is to prevent a conflict of interest and too much power being concentrated in the hands of one person. There is a strong parallel here with the structure of government, which tends to separate the political cabinet from the management civil service. In the United States, the board of directors (elected by the shareholders) is often equivalent to the supervisory board, while the executive board may often be known as the executive committee (the division/subsidiary heads and C-level officers that report directly to the CEO).

In other parts of the world, such as Asia, it is possible to have two or three *CEO*s in charge of one corporation. In the UK, many charities and government agencies are headed by a chief executive who is answerable to a board of trustees or board of directors. In the UK, similar to a sizable percentage of public companies in the US, the chair(person) (of the board) in public companies is more senior than the chief executive (who is usually known as the managing director). Most public companies now split the roles of chair and chief executive.

In the United States, and in business, the executive officers are usually the top officers of a corporation, the chief executive officer (CEO) being the best-known type. The definition varies; for instance, the California Corporate Disclosure Act defines "Executive Officers" as the five most highly-compensated officers not also sitting on the board of directors.

In the case of a sole proprietorship, an executive officer is the sole proprietor. In the case of a partnership, an executive officer is a managing partner, senior partner, or administrative partner. In the case of a limited liability company, an executive officer is any member, manager, or officer.

Structure

Typically, a CEO has several subordinate executives, each of whom has specific functional responsibilities. Common associates include a chief business development officer (CBDO), chief financial officer (CFO), chief operating officer (COO), chief marketing officer (CMO), chief information officer (CIO), chief communications officer (CCO), chief legal officer (CLO), chief technical officer (CTO), chief risk officer (CRO), chief creative officer (CCO), chief compliance officer (CCO), chief audit executive (CAE), chief diversity officer (CDO), or chief human resources officer (CHRO).

In hospitals and healthcare organizations, this also often includes a chief medical officer (CMO), a chief nursing officer (CNO), and a chief medical informatics officer (CMIO).

In the United Kingdom, the term 'director' is used instead of 'chief officer'. Associates include the audit executive, business development director, chief executive, compliance director, creative director, director of communications, diversity director, financial director, human resources director, information technology director, legal affairs director, managing director (MD), marketing director, operations director and technical director.

The UK is brimming with tourist attractions and holiday getaways, which in turn means that the hospitality business is a steadfast sector in which to work. If you've ever had designs on running your own bed & breakfast, or think that a career in hospitality is for you, then perhaps it's time to see if you've really got what it takes to make the change.

Running Your Own B&B

Running a bed and breakfast is hard work, but brings with it many benefits and rewards. For instance, you are often able to choose how many hours, days or weeks a year you work. You'll also have the chance to meet lots of interesting people.

But before you open your doors to tourists, holidaymaker's and businessmen, there are a few fundamental considerations you'll have to make to rectify whether you have what it takes to run your own bed and breakfast.

The first consideration is whether you would consider yourself physically fit enough to run your own establishment. Unless you're lucky enough to employ a cleaner or housekeeping staff, you may have to undertake daily chores for not only your living quarters, but to a high standard in your guest's quarters. Housekeeping skills will have to be impressive! Daily chores will most likely include tasks such as cleaning, cooking and laundry. Your working hours may also be long, with early starts to ensure breakfast meals are ready, often during weekends as well as festive and bank holidays.

You will also have to take into account your personal skills, as you may be playing host in your own home to people with difficult or challenging personalities! Diplomacy, patience, politeness and confidence are all beneficial qualities when running your own bed and breakfast establishment. Your hospitality skills will have to include meeting and greeting, dealing with any problems or enquiries, taking bookings, handling fees, as well as a high-quality culinary skills.

Business and Regulations

Inevitably, running a B&B will mean that you'll be handling the business, finance and marketing side of things. You'll need to understand your demographic and its requirements, as well as ways to obtain star rating awards. You'll also need to have sound IT skills to help you keep on top of Internet marketing, your accounts, bookings and general business administration.

You should also make yourself aware of the implications of opening your home to the public – there are stringent legal requirements that you'll have to adhere to. These include fire risk assessments, food hygiene and health & safety audits. You may also have to take into consideration aspects of the Disability Discrimination Act. The 'Pink Booklet' is available to help you understand why and how you can comply with the relevant legislation.

If you require some venture capital, then you'll have to formulate a business plan to approach your lender (usually a bank) with. To devise a viable business plan, you'll need to have undertaken relevant research, present evidence to back up your financial projections, which will include setting realistic prices and anticipating outgoings. You may need to enlist the help of an accountant, which will add to start up and running costs of your B&B.

If you're generally a friendly and confident person, and you think you can take on all the different challenging aspects of running a bed and breakfast, then you are already on the road to making a viable lifestyle and career change.

Career Change - Hotel Manager

If you'd like to work in hospitality, but want more distance between work and home, then perhaps you've considered working as a hotel manager. In smaller hotels, a manager will usually be responsible for overseeing all aspects of the running of the hotel, from finances and staff supervision to dealing with issues such as security, buildings maintenance, regulations and licensing.

Managers often help out in dining room restaurants and bar areas during the quieter periods, usually during the day. You may also have the opportunity to live in-house. In larger hotels and hotel chains, managers may be responsible for just one aspect of the running of the hotel, and work under the supervision of a general manager. Hotel chain managers are often expected to deal with the larger corporate clients, conferences and entertainment bookings.

Personal Skills and Qualifications

Because of the diverse nature of managing a hotel, you'll need to have the appropriate skills to help you successfully carry out your job roles. You'll be dealing with customers and clients, so your communication, tact and mediation skills must be well honed, and your motivation and enthusiasm clear to see. You'll also need organisational skills, as well as some business acumen. You may be working under pressure and in a constantly busy environment, so you must be able to problem solve quickly and stay level headed in difficult situations.

To work in a more senior position in a hotel in a role such as manager, you may be able to start at a more junior level and work your way towards a managerial position. However, the chances are that you'll need to have either relevant employment experience (such as marketing) where you have demonstrated that you have all the skills to undertake this role, or an appropriate qualification.

There are many hospitality qualifications available, allowing you to pick and choose your method of study. For instance, you can undertake a full-time pertinent degree, BTEC HNC/HND or postgraduate course, and apply for management jobs once you've graduated. Alternatively, you can undertake a two-year hospitality-related foundation degree course that will allow you to work and support yourself in your free time in relevant employment.

Multi-task Role of Hotel Managers

Hotel managers oversee all aspects of running a hotel, from housekeeping and general maintenance to budget management and marketing.

Large hotels may have a manager for each department, reporting to the general manager. In smaller hotels, the manager is more involved in the day-to-day running of the hotel, often dealing directly with guests.

As a hotel manager, your tasks would typically include:

- setting annual budgets
- analyzing financial information and statistics
- setting business targets and marketing strategies
- managing staff
- organizing building maintenance
- making sure security is effective
- dealing with customer complaints and comments
- making sure the hotel follows regulations such as licensing laws
- securing corporate bookings for entertainment and conference facilities.

In larger hotels you will spend a lot of time in meetings with the heads of departments.

Hours

Your working hours will include evenings, weekends and public holidays. You will usually work shifts, including split shifts, especially as a junior manager.

In a small hotel you might help out in the bar or restaurant during the day. You may have the option to live in at the hotel.

Income

- Trainee and assistant hotel managers can earn around £17,000 a year.
- Managers of small hotels or deputy managers of larger ones can earn from £20,000 to around £35,000.
- Senior or general managers can earn £60,000 or more.

Figures are intended as a guideline only.

Entry Requirements

You could become a hotel manager in either of the following ways:

- working your way up to management level from a more junior position
- entering management after completing a BTEC HNC/HND, degree or postgraduate qualification.

Relevant degree and HNC/HND subjects include:

- Hospitality Management
- International Hospitality Management
- Hotel and Hospitality Management
- Hospitality and Licensed Retail Management.

You can also complete foundation degrees in subjects such as Hospitality Business Management. These are vocational courses that are usually studied over two years. You can study part-time whilst in relevant employment or full-time with work placements.

To search for foundation degrees, HNDs and degrees see the UCAS website.

If you have a degree you may be able to join a graduate management training scheme run by a hotel chain.

You may be able to get into this job through an Apprenticeship scheme. The range of Apprenticeships available in your area will depend on the local jobs market and the types of skills employers need from their workers. To find out more about Apprenticeships, visit the Apprenticeships website.

Training and Development

Once you are working as a hotel manager, you will usually train on the job, gaining experience in all aspects of the hotel.

You may be able to start at a lower level, such as administrator or department manager, and work towards qualifications including:

- NVQ Level 2 in Multi-Skilled Hospitality Services
- NVQ Level 3 in Hospitality Supervision.

By joining the Institute of Hospitality, you will have access to seminars, networking events and opportunities for continuing professional development (CPD). Check the Institute's website for details.

Skills and Knowledge

- business skills
- the ability to manage staff
- good written and spoken communication skills
- tact and diplomacy
- the ability to keep calm under pressure and solve problems quickly
- energy and enthusiasm
- good organisational skills.

Opportunities

You could work in hotels all over the UK. With some large hotel chains you could also have the opportunity to work abroad. If you start as a trainee with a hotel chain you will need to be prepared to travel to different areas of the country.

Your prospects for progression will depend on the size of the hotel, your experience and whether you are willing to move around the country. As an experienced manager you could open your own hotel.

In hotel chains, you may be able to specialise in areas such as marketing or training, perhaps after completing further qualifications.

Event Management

Event management is the application of project management to the creation and development of festivals, events and conferences. Event management involves studying the intricacies of the brand, identifying the target audience, devising the event concept, planning the logistics and coordinating the technical aspects before actually executing the modalities of the proposed event. Post-event analysis and ensuring a return on investment have become significant drivers for the event industry.

The recent growth of festivals and events as an industry around the world means that the management can no longer be *ad hoc*. Events and festivals, such as the Asian Games, have a large impact on their communities and, in some cases, the whole country.

The industry now includes events of all sizes from the Olympics down to a breakfast meeting for ten business people. Many industries, charitable organizations, and interest groups will hold events of some size in order to market themselves, build business relationships, raise money or celebrate.

MARKETING TOOL

Services

Event management companies and organizations service a variety of areas including corporate events (product launches, press conferences, corporate meetings and conferences), marketing programs (road shows, grand opening events), and special corporate hospitality events like concerts, award ceremonies, film premieres, launch/release parties, fashion shows, commercial events, private (personal) events such as weddings and bar mitzvahs.

Clients hire event management companies to handle a specific scope of services for the given event, which at its maximum may include all creative, technical and logistical elements of the event. (Or just a subset of these, depending on the client's needs, expertise and budget).

Event Manager

The event manager is the person who plans and executes the event. Event managers and their teams are often behind-the-scenes running the event. Event managers may also be involved in more than just the planning and execution of the event, but also brand building, marketing and communication strategy.

The event manager is an expert at the creative, technical and logistical elements that help an event succeed. This includes event design, audio-visual production, scriptwriting, logistics, budgeting, negotiation and, of course, client service. It is a multi-dimensional profession.

The event manager may become involved at the early initiation stages of the event. If the event manager has budget responsibilities at this early stage they may be termed an event or production executive. The early stages include:

- Site surveying
- Client Service
- Brief clarification
- Budget drafting
- Cash flow management
- Supply chain identification
- Procurement
- Scheduling
- Site design
- Technical design
- Health & Safety

An event manager who becomes involved closer to the event will often have a more limited brief. The key disciplines closer to the event are:

- Health & Safety including crowd management,
- Logistics
- Rigging
- Sound
- Light
- Video
- Detailed scheduling
- Security

As an Industry

Event Management is a multi-million dollar industry, growing rapidly, with mega shows and events hosted regularly.

Surprisingly, there is no formalized research conducted to assess the growth of this industry. The industry includes fields such as the MICE (Meetings, Incentives, Conventions and Exhibitions), conferences and seminars as well as live music and sporting events.

The logistics side of the industry is paid less than the sales/ sponsorship side, though some may say that these are two different industries.

Technology

Event management software companies provide event planners with software toois to handle many common activities such as delegate registration, hotel booking, travel booking or allocation of exhibition floorspace.

Education

There are an increasing number of universities which offer courses in event management, including diplomas and graduate degrees. In addition to these academic courses, there are many associations and societies that provide courses on the various aspects of the industry. Study includes organizational skills, technical knowledge, P.R., marketing, advertising, catering, logistics, decor, glamour identity, human relations, study of law and licenses, risk management, budgeting, study of allied industries like television, other media and several other areas.

Certification can be acquired from various sources to obtain designations such as Certified Trade Show Marketer (CTSM), Certified Manager of Exhibits (CME), Certified in Exhibition Management (CEM), Global Certification in Meeting Management (CMM), Certified Meeting Professional (CMP), Diploma in Event Management(DEM), Post Graduate Diploma in Event Management (PGDEM) and the Certified Special Event Professional (CSEP).

Career opportunities are in the following Industries :

1. Event Management

2. Event Management Consultancy
3. Hotel, travel and hospitality Industries
4. Advertising Agencies
5. Public Relations Firms
6. Corporations
7. News Media
8. Non-profit organization
9. Integrated Marketing & Communications
10. Event Budgeting and Accounting

CATEGORIES OF EVENTS

Events can be classified into four broad categories based on their purpose and objective:

1. Leisure events e.g. leisure sport, music, recreation.
2. Cultural events e.g. ceremonial, religious, art, heritage, and folklore.
3. Personal events e.g. weddings, birthdays, anniversaries.
4. Organizational events e.g. commercial, political, charitable, sales, product launch,expo.

How to Become a Hotel General Manager?

Leadership, good decision-maker, work well with a variety of people

Many people want to transfer their management skills over to a Hotel General Manager position. It's possible, but you will have to get some practical knowledge first.

Enjoy some great dining experiences in the hotel business—There are two ways: One start at the front desk and learn the ropes. chances are you will move up quickly if you have good leadership skills and a solid business background. However, most of us can't afford the low pay at the front desk.

You get great deals on vacations in the hotel business—The better option is to start at the hotel sales manager level and earn 50-60K plus bonus. Hotel companies like to take sales people and groom them for General Manager positions because they know how to make money for the hotel. You can get the experience you need to become a hotel sales manager from www.aprinda.com The courses at www.aprinda.com only take 14-20 hours to complete on-line.

General Managers can typically get rooms for free at their sister properties

How to Be a Better Manager

Listed below are ten things you can do to become a better manager. Pick one. Do it today. Pick another one for tomorrow. In two weeks, you will be a better manager.

1. Select the best people—As a manager, you are only as good as the people on your team. Give yourself a better chance to succeed by picking the best people from the start.

Read Job Interview Questions to Ask to learn to be better at selecting the best candidate for the job.

2. Be a motivator—Human beings do things because we want to. Sometimes we want to because the consequences of not wanting to do something are unpleasant. However, most of the time we want to do things because of what we get out of it.

It's no different at work, people do good work for the pay, or the prestige, or the recognition. They do bad work because they want to take it easy and still get paid. They work really hard because they want to impress someone. To motivate your people better, figure out what they want and how you can give that to them for doing what you want them to do.

3. Build Your Team—It is not enough that people are motivated to succeed at work. They have to work together as a team to accomplish the group's objective. After all, if we just want them to all "do their own thing" we don't need you as a manager to mold them into a team, do we?

Here are some ways to improve your team building skills:

4. Be a Leader, Not Only a Manager—You have built the best team from the best employee available. You motivated them to peak performance. What is missing? Motivating a team is worthless unless you provide direction; unless you turn that motivation toward a goal and lead the team to it. It is the ability to lead others that truly sets a manager apart from their peers. Remember that leaders are found at all levels of the organization, so be one.

5. Improve as a Communicator—Communication may be the single most important skill of a manager. After all, all the others depend on it. You can't be a leader if you can't communicate your vision. You can't motivate people if they can't understand what you want. Communication skills can be improved through practice. Here are two exercises you can use to improve your ability to communicate effectively.

6. Get Better At Managing Money—To stay in business, a company has to make money. That means bringing money in the door and it means spending less than you bring in. Depending on your function in the organization, you may have more influence on one area or the other, but you need to understand both. You can help your company, your employees, and yourself be getting better at managing the company's money.

Don't be put off by the numbers, or by the fact that "it's math".

7. Get Better at Managing Time—The one thing you will probably have less of at work than money is time. The better you get at managing time, yours and others, the more effective you will be as a manager.

8. Improve Yourself—Don't focus so hard on your people that you forget about yourself. Identify the areas in which you are weak and improve them. The fact that you are reading this article shows you understand the concept. You need to put it into practice.

9. Practice Ethical Management—Enron-like scandals have really driven home the point about how important ethics is in business. If you want to avoid similar mistake.

10. Take a Break—You are less effective as a manager if you are over-stressed. You are less tolerant. You snap at people more. No one wants to be anywhere near you. Take a break. Give yourself a chance to relax and recharge your batteries. Your increased productivity when you return will more than make up for the time you take off. Have a good laugh or go lie on a beach somewhere.

Bottom Line

Management is a skill that can be learned. You can improve as a manager by working every day to get better. Bookmark this page and come back every day for the next two weeks. If you pick one subject each day, and work on improving in that area, you will be a better manager before you know it. And others will notice it too.

3

Decision-making Skills

Decision making can be regarded as the mental processes (cognitive process) resulting in the selection of a course of action among several alternative scenarios. Every decision making process produces a final choice.The output can be an action or an opinion of choice.

Human performance in decision terms has been the subject of active research from several perspectives. From a psychological perspective, it is necessary to examine individual decisions in the context of a set of needs, preferences an individual has and values they seek. From a cognitive perspective, the decision making process must be regarded as a continuous process integrated in the interaction with the environment. From a normative perspective, the analysis of individual decisions is concerned with the logic of decision making and rationality and the invariant choice it leads to.

Yet, at another level, it might be regarded as a problem solving activity which is terminated when a satisfactory solution is found. Therefore, decision making is a reasoning or emotional process which can be rational or irrational, can be based on explicit assumptions or tacit assumptions.

Logical decision-making is an important part of all science-based professions, where specialists apply their knowledge in a given area to making informed decisions. For example, medical decision making often involves making a diagnosis and selecting an appropriate treatment.

Some research using naturalistic methods shows, however, that in situations with higher time pressure, higher stakes, or increased ambiguities, experts use intuitive decision making rather than structured approaches, following a recognition primed decision approach to fit a set of indicators into the expert's experience and immediately arrive at a satisfactory course of action without weighing alternatives.

Recent robust decision efforts have formally integrated uncertainty into the decision making process. However, Decision Analysis, recognized and included uncertainties with a structured and rationally justifiable method of decision making since its conception in 1964.

A major part of decision making involves the analysis of a finite set of alternatives described in terms of some evaluative criteria. These criteria may be benefit or cost in nature. Then the problem might be to rank these alternatives in terms of how attractive they are to the decision maker(s) when all the criteria are considered simultaneously.

Another goal might be to just find the best alternative or to determine the relative total priority of each alternative (for instance, if alternatives represent projects competing for funds) when all the criteria are considered simultaneously. Solving such problems is the focus of multi-criteria decision analysis (MCDA) also known as multi-criteria decision making (MCDM). This area of decision making, although it is very old and has attracted the interest of many researchers and practitioners, is still highly debated as there are many MCDA / MCDM methods which may yield very different results when they are applied on exactly the same data.This leads to the formulation of a decision making paradox.

PROBLEM ANALYSIS VS. DECISION MAKING

It is important to differentiate between problem analysis and decision making. The concepts are completely separate from one another. Problem analysis must be done first, then the information gathered in that process may be used towards decision making.

Problem Analysis

- Analyze performance, what should the results be against what they actually are
- Problems are merely deviations from performance standards
- Problem must be precisely identified and described
- Problems are caused by some change from a distinctive feature
- Something can always be used to distinguish between what has and hasn't been effected by a cause
- Causes to problems can be deducted from relevant changes found in analyzing the problem
- Most likely cause to a problem is the one that exactly explains all the facts

Decision Making

- Objectives must first be established
- Objectives must be classified and placed in order of importance
- Alternative actions must be developed
- The alternative must be evaluated against all the objectives
- The alternative that is able to achieve all the objectives is the tentative decision
- The tentative decision is evaluated for more possible consequences
- The decisive actions are taken, and immediate actions are taken to prevent any adverse consequences from becoming problems and starting both systems (problem analysis and decision making) all over again

Everyday Techniques

Some of the decision-making techniques people use in everyday life include:

- Pros and Cons: Listing the advantages and disadvantages of each option, popularized by Plato and Benjamin Franklin
- Simple Prioritization: Choosing the alternative with the highest probability-weighted utility for each alternative (see Decision Analysis) or derivative Possibilianism: Acting on choices so as not to preclude alternative understandings of equal probability, including active exploration of novel possibilities and emphasis on the necessity of holding multiple positions at once if there is no available data to privilege one over the others.
- Satisficing: Accepting the first option that seems like it might achieve the desired result
- Acquiesce to a person in authority or an "expert", just following orders
- Flipism: Flipping a coin, cutting a deck of playing cards, and other random or coincidence methods
- Prayer, tarot cards, astrology, augurs, revelation, or other forms of divination

DECISION-MAKING STAGES

Developed by B. Aubrey Fisher, there are four stages that should be involved in all group decision making. These stages, or sometimes called phases, are important for the decision-making process to begin

Orientation stage- This phase is where members meet for the first time and start to get to know each other.

Conflict stage- Once group members become familiar with each other, disputes, little fights and arguments occur. Group members eventually work it out.

Emergence stage- The group begins to clear up vague opinions by talking about them.

Reinforcement stage- Members finally make a decision, while justifying themselves that it was the right decision.

DECISION-MAKING STEPS

When in an organization and faced with a difficult decision, there are several steps one can take to ensure the best possible solutions will be decided. These steps are put into seven effective ways to go about this decision making process (McMahon 2007).

The **first step**: Outline your goal and outcome. This will enable decision makers to see exactly what they are trying to accomplish and keep them on a specific path.

The **second step**: Gather data. This will help decision makers have actual evidence to help them come up with a solution.

The **third step**: Brainstorm to develop alternatives. Coming up with more than one solution ables you to see which one can actually work.

The **fourth step**: List pros and cons of each alternative. With the list of pros and cons, you can eliminate the solutions that have more cons than pros, making your decision easier.

The **fifth step**: Make the decision. Once you analyze each solution, you should pick the one that has many pros (or the pros that are most significant), and is a solution that everyone can agree with.

The **sixth step**: Immediately take action. Once the decision is picked, you should implement it right away.

The **seventh step**: Learn from, and reflect on the decision making. This step allows you to see what you did right and wrong when coming up, and putting the decision to use.

COGNITIVE AND PERSONAL BIASES

Biases can creep into our decision making processes. Many different people have made a decision about the same question (*e.g.* "Should I have a doctor look at this troubling breast cancer symptom I've discovered?" "Why did I ignore the evidence that the project was going over budget?") and then craft potential cognitive interventions aimed at improving decision making outcomes.

Below is a list of some of the more commonly debated cognitive biases.

- Selective search for evidence (a.k.a. Confirmation bias in psychology) (Scott Plous, 1993) – We tend to be willing to gather facts that support certain conclusions but disregard other facts that support different conclusions. Individuals who are highly defensive in this manner show significantly greater left prefrontal cortex activity as measured by EEG than do less defensive individuals.
- Premature termination of search for evidence – We tend to accept the first alternative that looks like it might work.
- Inertia – Unwillingness to change thought patterns that we have used in the past in the face of new circumstances.
- Selective perception – We actively screen-out information that we do not think is important. (See prejudice.) In one demonstration of this effect, discounting of arguments with which one disagrees (by judging them as untrue or irrelevant) was decreased by selective activation of right prefrontal cortex.
- Wishful thinking or optimism bias – We tend to want to see things in a positive light and this can distort our perception and thinking.
- Choice-supportive bias occurs when we distort our memories of chosen and rejected options to make the chosen options seem more attractive.
- Recency – We tend to place more attention on more recent information and either ignore or forget more distant information. (See semantic priming.) The opposite effect in the first set of data or other information is termed Primacy effect (Plous, 1993).

- Repetition bias – A willingness to believe what we have been told most often and by the greatest number of different sources.
- Anchoring and adjustment – Decisions are unduly influenced by initial information that shapes our view of subsequent information.
- Group think – Peer pressure to conform to the opinions held by the group.
- Source credibility bias – We reject something if we have a bias against the person, organization, or group to which the person belongs: We are inclined to accept a statement by someone we like. (See prejudice.)
- Incremental decision making and escalating commitment – We look at a decision as a small step in a process and this tends to perpetuate a series of similar decisions. This can be contrasted with **zero-based decision making**. (See slippery slope.)
- Attribution asymmetry – We tend to attribute our success to our abilities and talents, but we attribute our failures to bad luck and external factors. We attribute other's success to good luck, and their failures to their mistakes.
- Role fulfillment (Self Fulfilling Prophecy) – We conform to the decision making expectations that others have of someone in our position.
- Underestimating uncertainty and the illusion of control – We tend to underestimate future uncertainty because we tend to believe we have more control over events than we really do. We believe we have control to minimize potential problems in our decisions.

Reference class forecasting was developed to eliminate or reduce cognitive biases in decision making.

Post decision Analysis

Evaluation and analysis of past decisions is complementary to decision making; see also mental accounting.

Cognitive Styles

Influence of Briggs Myers Type

According to behavioralist Isabel Briggs Myers, a person's decision making process depends to a significant degree on their cognitive style. Myers developed a set of four bi-polar dimensions, called the Myers-Briggs Type Indicator (MBTI). The terminal points on these dimensions are: *thinking* and *feeling; extroversion* and *introversion; judgment* and *perception*; and *sensing* and *intuition*. She claimed that a person's decision making style correlates well with how they score on these four dimensions.

For example, someone who scored near the thinking, extroversion, sensing, and judgment ends of the dimensions would tend to have a logical, analytical, objective, critical, and empirical decision making style. However, some psychologists say that the MBTI lacks reliability and validity and is poorly constructed.

Other studies suggest that these national or cross-cultural differences exist across entire societies. For example, Maris Martinsons has found that American, Japanese and Chinese business leaders each exhibit a distinctive national style of decision making.

Optimizing vs. Satisficing

Herbert Simon coined the phrase "bounded rationality" to express the idea that human decision-making is limited by available information, available time, and the information-processing ability of the mind. Simon also defined two cognitive styles: *maximizers* try to make an optimal decision, whereas *satisficers* simply try to find a solution that is "good enough". Maximizers tend to take longer making decisions due to the need to maximize performance across all variables and make tradeoffs carefully; they also tend to more often regret their decisions.

Combinatoral vs. Positional

Styles and methods of decision making were elaborated by the founder of Predispositioning Theory, Aron

Katsenelinboigen. In his analysis on styles and methods Katsenelinboigen referred to the game of chess, saying that "chess does disclose various methods of operation, notably the creation of predisposition—methods which may be applicable to other, more complex systems."

In his book Katsenelinboigen states that apart from the methods (reactive and selective) and sub-methods (randomization, predispositioning, programming), there are two major styles – positional and combinational. Both styles are utilized in the game of chess. According to Katsenelinboigen, the two styles reflect two basic approaches to the uncertainty: deterministic (combinational style) and indeterministic (positional style). Katsenelinboigen's definition of the two styles are the following.

The combinational style is characterized by

- a very narrow, clearly defined, primarily material goal, and
- a program that links the initial position with the final outcome.

In defining the combinational style in chess, Katsenelinboigen writes:

The combinational style features a clearly formulated limited objective, namely the capture of material (the main constituent element of a chess position). The objective is implemented via a well defined and in some cases in a unique sequence of moves aimed at reaching the set goal. As a rule, this sequence leaves no options for the opponent. Finding a combinational objective allows the player to focus all his energies on efficient execution, that is, the player's analysis may be limited to the pieces directly partaking in the combination. This approach is the crux of the combination and the combinational style of play.

The positional style is distinguished by

- a positional goal and
- a formation of semi-complete linkages between the initial step and final outcome.

"Unlike the combinational player, the positional player is occupied, first and foremost, with the elaboration of the position that will allow him to develop in the unknown future. In playing the positional style, the player must evaluate relational and material parameters as independent variables. (...) The positional style gives the player the opportunity to develop a position until it becomes pregnant with a combination. However, the combination is not the final goal of the positional player—it helps him to achieve the desirable, keeping in mind a predisposition for the future development. The Pyrrhic victory is the best example of one's inability to think positionally."

The positional style serves to

(a) create a predisposition to the future development of the position;

(b) induce the environment in a certain way;

(c) absorb an unexpected outcome in one's favor;

(d) avoid the negative aspects of unexpected outcomes.

The positional style gives the player the opportunity to develop a position until it becomes pregnant with a combination. Katsenelinboigen writes:

"As the game progressed and defense became more sophisticated the combinational style of play declined. . . . The positional style of chess does not eliminate the combinational one with its attempt to see the entire program of action in advance. The positional style merely prepares the transformation to a combination when the latter becomes feasible."

NEUROSCIENCE PERSPECTIVE

The anterior cingulate cortex (ACC), orbitofrontal cortex (and the overlapping ventromedial prefrontal cortex) are brain regions involved in decision making processes. A recent neuroimaging study, found distinctive patterns of neural activation in these regions depending on whether decisions were made on the basis of personal volition or following directions from someone else. Patients with damage to the ventromedial prefrontal cortex have difficulty making advantageous decisions.

A recent study involving Rhesus monkeys found that neurons in the parietal cortex not only represent the formation of a decision but also signal the degree of certainty (or "confidence") associated with the decision. Another recent study found that lesions to the ACC in the macaque resulted in impaired decision making in the long run of reinforcement guided tasks suggesting that the ACC may be involved in evaluating past reinforcement information and guiding future action.

Emotion appears to aid the decision making process: Decision making often occurs in the face of uncertainty about whether one's choices will lead to benefit or harm (see also Risk). The somatic-marker hypothesis is a neurobiological theory of how decisions are made in the face of uncertain outcome.

This theory holds that such decisions are aided by emotions, in the form of bodily states, that are elicited during the deliberation of future consequences and that mark different options for behavior as being advantageous or disadvantageous. This process involves an interplay between neural systems that elicit emotional/bodily states and neural systems that map these emotional/bodily states.

Although it is unclear whether the studies generalize to all processing, there is evidence that volitional movements are initiated, not by the conscious decision making self, but by the subconscious.

Information Industry

Information industry or information industries are a loosely defined term for industries that are information intensive in one way or the other. It is considered one of the most important economic sectors for a variety of reasons.

There are many different kinds of information industries, and many different ways to classify them. Although there is no standard or distinctively better way of organizing those different views, the following section offers a review of what the term "information industry" might entail, and why. Following that is a review of alternative conceptualization such as knowledge industry and information-related occupation. The term is mostly identified with computer programming, system design, telecommunications, and others.

Types of Information Industries

First, there are companies which produce and sell information in form of good or service. Media products such as television programs and movies, published books and periodicals would constitute probably among the most accepted part of what information goods can be. Some information is provided not as a tangible commodity but as a service.

Consulting is among the least controversial of this kind. However, even for this category, disagreements can occur due to the vagueness of the term "information." For some, information is knowledge about a subject, something one can use to improve the performance of other activities—it does not include arts and entertainments.

For others, information is something that is mentally processed and consumed, either to improve other activities (such as production) or for personal enjoyment; it would include artists and architects. For yet others, information may include anything that has to do with sensation, and therefore information industries may include even such things as restaurant, amusement parks, and prostitution to the extent that food, park ride, and sexual intercourse have to do with senses. In spite of the definitional problems, industries producing information goods and services are called information industries.

Second, there are information processing services. Some services, such as legal services, banking, insurance, computer programming, data processing, testing, and market research, require intensive and intellectual processing of information. Although those services do not necessarily provide information, they often offer expertise in making decisions on behalf of clients. These kinds of service industries can be regarded as an information-intensive part of various industries that is externalized and specialized.

Third, there are industries that are vital to the dissemination of the information goods mentioned above. For example, telephone, broadcasting and book retail industries do not produce much information, but their core business is to disseminate information others produced. These industries handle predominantly information and can be distinguished from wholesale or retail industries in general.

It is just a coincidence, one can argue, that some of those industries are separately existing from the more obvious information-producing industries. For example, in the United States, as well as some other countries, broadcasting stations produce very limited amount of programs they broadcast. But this is not the only possible form of division of labor. If legal, economic, cultural, and historical circumstances were different, the broadcasters would have been the producers of their own programs.

Therefore, in order to capture the information related activities of the economy, it might be a good idea to include this type of industry. These industries show how much of an economy is about information, as opposed to materials. It is useful to differentiate production of valuable information from processing that information in a sophisticated way, from the movement of information.

Fourth, there are manufacturers of information-processing devices that require research and sophisticated decision-making. These products are vital to information-processing activities of above mentioned industries. The products include computers of various levels and many other microelectronic devices, as well as software programs. Printing and copying machines, measurement and recording devices of various kinds, electronic or otherwise, are also in this category.

The role of these tools are to automate certain information-processing activities. The use of some of these tools may be very simple (as in the case of some printing), and the processing done by the tools may be very simple (as in copying and some calculations) rather than intellectual and sophisticated.

In other words, the specialization of these industries in an economy is neither production of information nor sophisticated decision-making. Instead, this segment serves as an infrastructure for those activities, making production of information and decision-making services will be a lot less efficient.

In addition, these industries tend to be "high-tech" or research intensive - trying to find more efficient ways to boost efficiency of information production and sophisticated decision-making. For example, the function of a standard calculator is quite simple and it is easy to how to use it. However, manufacturing a well-functioning standard calculator takes a lot of processes, far more than the task of calculation performed by the users.

Fifth, there are very research-intensive industries that do not serve as infrastructure to information-production or sophisticated decision-making. Pharmaceutical, food-processing, some apparel design, and some other "high-tech" industries belong to this type. These products are not exclusively for information production or sophisticated decision-making, although many are helpful. Some services, such as medical examination are in this category as well. One can say these industries involve a great deal of sophisticated decision-making, although that part is combined with manufacturing or "non-informational" activities.

Finally, there are industries that are not research intensive, but serve as infrastructure for information production and sophisticated decision-making. Manufacturing of office furniture would be a good example, although it sometimes involves research in ergonomics and development of new materials.

As stated above, this rather long list of candidates for information industries is not a definitive way of organizing differences that researchers may pay attention to when they define the term. Among the difficulties is, for example, the position of advertising industry.

Importance of Information Industries

Information industries are considered important for several distinctive reasons. Even among the experts who think information industries are important, disagreements may exist regarding which reason to accept and which to reject.

First, information industries are a rapidly growing part of economy. The demand for information goods and services from consumers is increasing. In case of consumers, media including music and motion picture, personal computers, video game-related industries, are among the information industries.

In case of businesses, information industries include computer programming, system design, so-called FIRE (finance, insurance, and real estate) industries, telecommunications, and others. When demand for these industries are growing nationally or internationally, that creates an opportunity for an urban, regional, or national economy to grow rapidly by specializing on these sectors.

Second, information industries are considered to boost innovation and productivity of other industries. An economy with a strong information industry might be a more competitive one than others, other factors being equal.

Third, some believe that the effect of the changing economic structure (or composition of industries within an economy) is related to the broader social change. As information becomes the central part of our economic activities we evolve into an "information society", with an increased role of mass media, digital technologies, and other mediated information in our daily life, leisure activities, social life, work, politics, education, art, and many other aspects of society.

Market Research is Important to Business Decision-Making

The entrepreneur was in business for decades and made the decision to *"...play with the big guns in the bright lights of the city..."*.This decision opened up the opportunity to move the company's operations from a rural to an urban setting with new office location. However, the entrepreneur failed to obtain market data for the new location and did not survey the landscape into which the business was moving, a landscape which was heavily saturated with existing competitors with their own competitive niches and by the looks of things seemed very *"closed and unfriendly"* to new entrants. **Why then was the decision made to move the business into a new environment?**

The small business owner believed the company's **brand** and **loyal customer base** carried enough **good faith value** to guarantee its survival after the move, even in a sluggish economy. However, as presented in that article, "Why Hire A Virtual Assistant?...A Virtual Who", the outcome turned out to be quite different. The small business went under a little over a year after the move because the decision makers failed to engage in a comprehensive market analysis, assess the market into which it was running head long prior to the move, and or brainstorm alternative ideas and solutions to the issues and or problem motivating the move.

Prior to entering the market, the solo service professional should have conducted a **comprehensive market analysis**. Market analysis data help guide decision-makers into making informed decisions when **gauging the pulse or surveying the landscape of a particular market segment** into which they are heading. **Surveying the landscape** helps business owners **prepare to enter a new market, launch a new product** or **service**, or **grow a new start up** and or **existing business**. It also provides **valuable business intelligence** for decision makers when designing their product and services so they can effectively meet the demands and or needs of their target audience as well as **identify the market's attributes**. A market's attributes are those **elements** that are **characteristic** to a specific market such as:

1. Types of industries existing in the market or seeking to gain entrance, and the types of products and or services offerings available.
2. Size of the target industry, the number of competitors, their niches and unique selling proposition.
3. Market saturation or openness and feasibility for new entrants, and number of potential competitors, customers and their commonalities in the market space. Commonalities signals market and industry trends, behaviors and expectations for a new product or service entrant.
4. Observed market volatility or stability, allowance for innovation, rate at which small businesses are experiencing growth and how well they are doing overall.

When conducted thoroughly and accurately, the data gathered from a comprehensive market analysis can help determine if the market is **overly saturated, open to accepting new ideas, products, services and or new business owners and to what degree is differentiation and innovation in product and service or delivery facilitated.**

Hiring a Virtual Assistant/Virtual Office Assistant (VA/VOA), skilled in **market research** and **analysis, competitor analysis**, and or **small business development** would have been a great solution and investment for this solo service professional portrayed in "Why Hire A Virtual Assistant?...A Virtual Who". As you may recall cost was a huge influencing factor in the decision to abandon the idea of conducting a comprehensive market reseach analysis. While there are no guarantees when implementing such a business strategy, the services of an independent virtual market research analyst, competitor market analyst and or small business development service professional or consultant would have allowed this small business portrayed in "Why Hire A Virtual Assistant?...A Virtual Who", the opportunity to **leverage** scarce available

resources to help achieve the desired outcome – transitioning from a rural to an urban market environment, thereby lessening the impact of the decision to move a rural based business into a highly competitive urban atmosphere.

Decision-making is an important process for organizational effectiveness. Decision making is almost universally defined as choosing between alternatives. It is closely related to all the traditional management functions. In the manufacturing area, effective decisions are aimed at achieving zero defects in recent years this focus has also been applied to the service sector in order to create zero defections. Decision making is an organizational process because it transcends the individual and has an effect on organizational goals. First the overall nature of the decision making is explored.

Then the models of behavioural decision making are described. Next, the traditional and modern participative techniques are presented as behaviourally oriented decision techniques. Creativity in decision making can apply to individuals or groups. Since individual decision making has largely given way to group decision making in today, organizations, an understanding of group dynamics become relevant. In fast a no of social decision schemes have emerged.

Decisions can be classified as either programmed or non-programmed. Programmed decisions are repetitive or routine and can be solved through clear-cut mechanical procedures, such as applying the rules to find the best solution. Up to 90 percent of management decisions are programmed. Non-programmed decisions are exceptional or non-recurring, and they are often made under crisis conditions which involve so much ambiguity that specific procedures or programs are not available. Therefore, managers who must make non-programmed decisions rely on judgement and creativity.

How to Make an Important Decision

Making decisions can be extremely difficult. It's easy to get lost in what should or should not be done or wrapped up in emotions rather than actually making the decision. Your agenda needs to be healthy decision making. When you have something important to decide then try this strategy (which actually works for small or big decisions).

Okay, you have a decision to make. Get out a piece of paper. On one side of the paper write down the pros or positive outcome of making your choice. What are the benefits, or positive results that may occur from this decision?

On the other side of the paper write down the cons to this decision. Why should you not make this choice, and if you do make it, what are the possible negative consequences?

Of course, you can write it out however you need to do it whether it's on the computer or making columns just as long as you're able to clearly see both the positive and negative of the decision. Make sure to be as exhaustive that you need to in order to make your decision.

Evaluate the whole picture. Look at everything you have written down, weighing it, and give yourself some time to make your choice. It's a simple decision making process, but that does not mean your choice is going to be easy.

Here's an example. It's a complicated issue that is being overly simplified. Should I file bankruptcy?

Pros: don't have the money to pay off debt, will be able to start over, will be able to obtain credit, doesn't look good on credit report but no worse than repeated delinquency, debt to income ratio is too high

Cons: black mark on credit report, costs money to file, not everything can be discharged (student loans), want to pay off debt responsibly, feel guilty

4

CORDIAL WORK CLIMATE

Teamwork is important in it and is also the best way to develop the specific leadership qualities needed for the hospitality industry. We are so convinced of the value of group work that student teams are coached and guided in how to work successfully together. Coaching will help you learn to listen to others – and also to be attentive to what they are not saying. You will see when teams work, and when they don't.

TEAMWORK AND THE WORKPLACE

In the workplace currently, there is a tendency to move away from top-down decision making and to give more responsibility down the line. At the same time, companies are relying more and more on work done by self-directed work groups. We put an emphasis on teamwork and require a large number of projects to be carried out in teams, with the result that students leaving the school have had considerable experience in this field and are thus better prepared for their future employment. Companies who come on campus to recruit EHL students say that they particularly appreciate their flexibility and their ability to work in teams.

Skills Developed by Group Work

Skills developed by group work include analytical and cognitive skills, collaborative skills, such as conflict management, flexibility, negotiation and compromise, organization and time management skills, problem solving...The fact that the school is multi-cultural (and multi-lingual) adds an extra challenge. Different values, often linked with the cultural aspect, can be another source of conflict. What better way to learn leadership skills for hospitality?

Students are assigned to groups - mirroring the workplace, where they will not be able to choose their co-workers - and the groups are regularly changed to give them plenty of experience of group dynamics.

Frustrations... and Satisfaction

While working on projects, students learn at the same time to evaluate their own behaviour within the group to understand whether it contributes or not to the task in hand. Group work can be a source of anything from great satisfaction (professional and personal) and pleasure, to a situation causing extreme frustration, disappointment and even anger. Very often it is the "natural leaders" who experience the most frustration - and as at EHL most students have leadership qualities, there is a lot to learn!

Whatever the outcome, the individual student receives a very valuable learning experience and most report that they are pleased with their group work.

An organization doesn't thrive on its lofty vision and far reaching ideas alone. It depends a lot on how the managers and executives manage the workforce so that they give in their best. An organization where the workers work like the cogs in a wheel is sure to be a success, and even carry the success forward. Naturally, it would be foolhardy to assume that only a heavy package would make the employees run to push the company forward. Employees should be nurtured; they should be taken care of so that they feel a part of the organization. And the employers should accept the fact that from time to time even the best employees should be encouraged. A simple pat on the back can go a long way in boosting the morale of the employee. Employee motivation is an unwritten characteristic in the job profile of managers and executives.

That is why it is very important that employers know how to motivate their workforce, if they want better productivity. There are many ways in which employees can be motivated and some of the most effective ideas are listed below.

Ways To Motivate Employees

- Employers should remember that every achievement of the employee should be met with appreciation and recognition. The employee should know that he/she has the attention of the higher ups. This will motivate the employee to achieve more, as he/she will see that the work being done is noticed.
- Another form of recognition and a very effective one is to physically applaud the employee. A round of applause for an achievement will not only boost the morale of the employee, but it will also make him/her feel proud to work in an organization, where his/her work is applauded. For applause the workers should not wait for a specific occasion. Applaud wherever and whenever and it will always be appreciated.
- Job title is another great employee motivating idea. And this perhaps has the most lasting impression. Job title leaves a positive impression on the self esteem of the employee. The reason job title is such an effective motivating factor is because it makes the employee feel proud of how he/she is perceived in the organization by the other workers and the employers.
- Employee motivation depends a lot on how good the work environment is. It is very important that the working conditions be employee-friendly or soon they will get bored and demotivated with the work. Naturally, the productivity will go down. Thus, the working condition is also a major cause of attrition.
- Employers should cultivate team spirit among the staff. A team where all the workers gel along comfortably will always be productive and the employee will stay motivated to work harder. A team should be made to

feel like a family and it is very necessary to make every employee feel that he/she is an integral part of this family.

- Taking all the employees to any off site event is also very beneficial. Such a social gathering fosters bonding among the coworkers, which ultimately has a positive effect on the morale of the employee. Celebrating festivals and company events is the best way to engage in social gathering. This is also a very good way for the employer to interact with the staff in a casual atmosphere.
- The best employee motivator for all is monetary compensation. A hike from time to time is a great motivator. Monetary compensation can also be in the form of special gifts and vouchers that can be given to different employees either monthly or weekly according to the fancy of the employer.

ECO-FRIENDLY HOTELS

Looking to explore a new place and help to save the environment on your next vacation? The travel industry has heard your demand and adapted. Eco-friendly hotels have sprung up around the world offering guests a more green way to vacation. Gabe Saglie, senior editor at Travelzoo, said that while more travelers are becoming environmentally-conscious, many do not stay at green hotels due to the cumbersome process of researching hotels' eco-practices. Others said it is difficult to find green hotels within their budgets.

So for Earth Day's 40th anniversary Travelzoo put together a list of outstanding eco-certified hotel deals .

All of the properties have been LEED-certified, which means they fit the U.S. Green Building Council's standards for Leadership in Energy and Environmental Design, or LEED.

The building council's program evaluates hotels for sustainable site development, water savings, energy efficiency, materials selection and indoor environmental quality to ensure a whole-building approach to sustainability. LEED certification provides independent, third-party verification for environmentally responsible hotels.

Here are six of the best deals at environmentally-friendly hotels from Travelzoo:

The Avalon Hotel & Spa, Portland, Ore.: This elegant boutique property was Oregon's first hotel to receive LEED Silver Certification. The hotel is perched along the Willamette River and inside Cottonwood Bay, a protected green area and features its own protected natural area (which doubles as a butterfly refuge), a full-service spa and upscale Italian restaurant. Through April, the hotel is offering rooms from $84 a night, 40 percent off the normal rate. The deal includes free breakfast for two and 20 percent off spa services.

Performance Management

Performance management (PM) includes activities that ensure that goals are consistently being met in an effective and efficient manner. Performance management can focus on the performance of an organization, a department, employee, or even the processes to build a product or service, as well as many other areas.

Performance management as referenced on this page is a broad term coined by Dr. Aubrey Daniels in the late 1970s to describe a technology (i.e. science imbedded in applications methods) for managing both behavior and results, two critical elements of what is known as performance.

Application

This is used most often in the workplace, can apply wherever people interact — schools, churches, community meetings, sports teams, health setting, governmental agencies, and even political settings - anywhere in the world people interact with their environments to produce desired effects. Armstrong and Baron (1998) defined it as a "strategic and integrated approach to increasing the effectiveness of organizations by improving the performance of the people who work in them and by developing the capabilities of teams and individual contributors."

It may be possible to get all employees to reconcile personal goals with organizational goals and increase productivity and profitability of an organization using this process. It can be applied by organisations or a single department or section inside an organisation, as well as an individual person. The performance process is appropriately named the self-propelled performance process (SPPP).

First, a commitment analysis must be done where a job mission statement is drawn up for each job. The job mission statement is a job definition in terms of purpose, customers, product and scope. The aim with this analysis is to determine the continuous key objectives and performance standards for each job position.

Following the commitment analysis is the work analysis of a particular job in terms of the reporting structure and job description. If a job description is not available, then a systems analysis can be done to draw up a job description. The aim with this analysis is to determine the continuous critical objectives and performance standards for each job.

Benefits

Managing employee or system performance facilitates the effective delivery of strategic and operational goals. There is a clear and immediate correlation between using performance management programs or software and improved business and organizational results.

For employee performance management, using integrated software, rather than a spreadsheet based recording system, may deliver a significant return on investment through a range of direct and indirect sales benefits, operational efficiency benefits and by unlocking the latent potential in every employees work day (i.e. the time they spend not actually doing their job). Benefits may include:

Direct Financial Gain

- Grow sales
- Reduce costs in the organisation
- Stop project overruns
- Aligns the organization directly behind the CEO's goals
- Decreases the time it takes to create strategic or operational changes by communicating the changes through a new set of goals

Motivated Workforce

- Optimizes incentive plans to specific goals for over achievement, not just business as usual
- Improves employee engagement because everyone understands how they are directly contributing to the organisations high level goals
- Create transparency in achievement of goals
- High confidence in bonus payment process
- Professional development programs are better aligned directly to achieving business level goals

Improved Management Control

- Flexible, responsive to management needs
- Displays data relationships
- Helps audit / comply with legislative requirements
- Simplifies communication of strategic goals scenario planning
- Provides well documented and communicated process documentation

ORGANIZATIONAL DEVELOPMENT

In organizational development (OD), *performance* can be thought of as Actual Results vs Desired Results. Any discrepancy, where Actual is less than Desired, could constitute the performance improvement zone. Performance management and improvement can be thought of as a cycle:

1. Performance planning where goals and objectives are established
2. Performance coaching where a manager intervenes to give feedback and adjust performance
3. Performance appraisal where individual performance is formally documented and feedback delivered

A performance problem is any gap between Desired Results and Actual Results. Performance improvement is any effort targeted at closing the gap between Actual Results and Desired Results.

Other organizational development definitions are slightly different. The U.S. Office of Personnel Management (OPM) indicates that Performance Management consists of a system or process whereby:

1. Work is planned and expectations are set
2. Performance of work is monitored
3. Staff ability to perform is developed and enhanced
4. Performance is rated or measured and the ratings summarized
5. Top performance is rewarded

Comforting Zone

People travel for a variety of reasons, including for vacations, business, and visits to friends and relatives. For many of these travelers, hotels and other accommodations will be where they stay while out of town. For others, hotels may be more than just a place to stay; they are destinations in themselves. Resort hotels and casino hotels, for example, offer a variety of activities to keep travelers and families occupied for much of their stay.

Hotels and other accommodations are as different as the many family and business travelers they accommodate. The industry includes all types of lodging, from luxurious five-star hotels to youth hostels and RV (recreational vehicle) parks. While many provide simply a place to spend the night, others cater to longer stays by providing food service, recreational activities, and meeting rooms. In 2008, 64,300 establishments provided accommodations to suit many different needs and budgets.

A work climate is the workplace environment. Business climates affect how well company goals are being met because maximum efficiency, production and employee motivation are impossible when the work climate is poor. Effective work climates ensure that employees are clear about their purpose in the larger realm of the company and know exactly what is expected of them. In this way, companies can better function as a whole to meet their goals.

In a poor work climate such as one of ineffective communication and unfocused supervision, the productive goals can become unclear. Employees may lack interest or motivation which is likely to decrease productivity even further. Even if employees are still productive, it may be wasted if they are working on tasks that don't fit into crucial company goals. In this way, a good work climate is one that is supported and enhanced by effective management.

Business climates that work with employees to set and achieve clear goals can be very successful. This is one reason why performance management is so important in many companies today. Regular performance reviews can help motivate employees to keep improving as well as remind them exactly what tasks are expected of them within the work climate. Incentives such as raises, promotions and bonuses for jobs well done further motivate employees to continue their best efforts in the workplace.

Just as weather climates affect people who live in them, the same can be said about a work climate. Healthy, communicative work environments support an efficient work force that is ready to commit daily to its assigned tasks to keep the company running profitably. A poor work climate, on the other hand, doesn't support a strong, motivated team environment.

Ultimately, positive work climates can drastically reduce employee turnover rates by retaining more employees. Healthy, happy employees are likely to stay in a company longer. High employee turnover rates can be damaging to a business because too much time and resources may be needed such as constantly hiring and training new staff. Employees in a positive work climate often go above and beyond their job description to help the company thrive.

Hotels and motels comprise the majority of establishments in this industry and are generally classified as offering either full-service or limited service. Full-service properties offer a variety of services for their guests, but they almost always include at least one or more restaurant and beverage service options other than self-service—from coffee bars and lunch counters to cocktail lounges and formal restaurants. They also usually provide room service. Larger full-service properties usually have a variety of retail shops on the premises, such as gift boutiques, newsstands, and drug and cosmetics counters, some of which may be geared to an exclusive clientele. Additionally, a number of full-service hotels offer guests access to laundry and valet services, swimming pools, beauty salons, and fitness centers or health spas. A small—but growing—number of luxury hotel chains also manage condominium units in combination with their transient rooms, providing both hotel guests and condominium owners with access to the same services and amenities.

The largest hotels often have banquet rooms, exhibit halls, and spacious ballrooms to accommodate conventions, business meetings, wedding receptions, and other social gatherings. Conventions and business meetings are major sources of revenue for these properties. Some commercial hotels are known as conference hotels—fully self-contained entities specifically designed for large-scale meetings. They provide physical fitness and recreational facilities for meeting attendees, in addition to state-of-the-art audiovisual and technical equipment, a business center, and banquet services.

Limited-service hotels are free-standing properties that do not have on-site restaurants or most other amenities that must be provided by a staff other than the front desk or housekeeping. They usually offer continental breakfasts, vending machines or small packaged items, Internet access, and sometimes unattended game rooms or swimming pools in addition to daily housekeeping services. The numbers of limited-service properties have been growing. These properties are not as costly to build and maintain. They appeal to budget-conscious family vacationers and travelers who are willing to sacrifice amenities for lower room prices.

Hotels can also be categorized based on a distinguishing feature or service provided by the hotel. *Conference hotels* provide meeting and banquet rooms, and usually food service, to large groups of people. *Resort hotels* offer luxurious surroundings with a variety of recreational facilities, such as swimming pools, golf courses, tennis courts, game rooms, and health spas, as well as planned social activities and entertainment. Resorts typically are located in vacation destinations or near natural settings, such as mountains, seashores, theme parks, or other attractions. As a result, the business of many resorts fluctuates with the season. Some resort hotels and motels provide additional convention and conference facilities to encourage customers to combine business with pleasure. During the off season, many of these establishments solicit conventions, sales meetings, and incentive tours to fill their otherwise empty rooms; some resorts even close for the off-season.

Extended-stay hotels typically provide rooms or suites with fully equipped kitchens, entertainment systems, office space with computer and telephone lines, fitness centers, and other amenities. Typically, guests use these hotels for a minimum of 5 consecutive nights, often while on an extended work assignment or lengthy vacation or family visit. *All-suite hotels* offer a living room or sitting room in addition to a bedroom.

Casino hotels combine both lodging and legalized gaming on the same premises. Along with the typical services provided by most full-service hotels, casino hotels also contain casinos where patrons can wager at table games, play slot machines, and make other bets. Some casino hotels also contain conference and convention facilities.

In addition to hotels, *bed-and-breakfast inns, RV parks, campgrounds,* and *rooming and boarding houses* provide lodging for overnight guests and are included in this industry. *Bed-and-breakfast inns* provide short-term lodging in private homes or small buildings converted for this purpose and are characterized by highly personalized service and inclusion of breakfast in the room rate. Their appeal is quaintness; they typically provide unusual service and unique decor.

RV parks and campgrounds cater to people who enjoy recreational camping at moderate prices. Some parks and campgrounds provide service stations, general stores, shower and toilet facilities, and coin-operated laundries. While some are designed for overnight travelers only, others are for vacationers who stay longer. Some camps provide accommodations, such as cabins and fixed campsites, and other amenities, such as food services, recreational facilities and equipment, and organized recreational activities. Examples of these overnight camps include children's camps, family vacation camps, hunting and fishing camps, and outdoor adventure retreats that offer trail riding, white-water rafting, hiking, fishing, game hunting, and similar activities.

Other short-term lodging facilities in this industry include *guesthouses,* or small cottages located on the same property as a main residence, and *youth hostels*—dormitory-style hotels with few frills, occupied mainly by students traveling on limited budgets. Also included are *rooming and boarding houses,* such as fraternity houses, sorority houses, off-campus dormitories, and workers' camps. These establishments provide temporary or longer term accommodations that may serve as a principal residence for the period of occupancy. These establishments also may provide services such as housekeeping, meals, and laundry services.

In recent years, the hotel industry has been dominated by a few large national hotel chains. To the traveler, familiar chain establishments represent dependability and quality at predictable rates. Many chains recognize the importance of brand loyalty to guests and have expanded the range of lodging options offered under one corporate name to include a full range of hotels from limited-service, economy-type hotels to luxury inns. While these national corporations own some of the hotels, many properties are independently owned but affiliated with a chain through a franchise agreement or management contract. Increasingly, hotel chains are moving away from owning properties to managing them. As part of a chain, individual hotels can participate in the company's national reservations service or incentive program, thereby appearing to belong to a larger enterprise.

For those who prefer more personalized service and a unique experience, *boutique hotels* are becoming more popular. These smaller hotels are generally found in urban locations and provide patrons good service and more distinctive decor and food selection.

Although there are nationwide RV parks and campgrounds, most small lodging establishments are individually owned and operated by a single owner, who may employ a small staff to help operate the business.

The lodging industry is moving towards more limited-service properties mostly in suburban, residential, or commercial neighborhoods, often locating hotels near popular restaurants. Many full-service properties are limiting or quitting the food service business altogether, choosing to contract out their food service operations to third party restaurateurs, including long-term arrangements with chain restaurant operators. Urban business and entertainment districts are providing a greater mix of lodging options to appeal to a wider range of travelers.

Increased competition among establishments in this industry has spurred many independently owned and operated hotels and other lodging places to join national or international reservation systems. This allows travelers to make multiple reservations for lodging, airlines, and car rentals with one telephone call or Internet search. Nearly all hotel chains and many independent lodging facilities operate online reservation systems through the Internet or maintain Web sites that allow individuals to book rooms. Online marketing of properties is so popular with guests that many hotels promote themselves with elaborate Web sites and allow people to investigate availability and rates.

Because hotels are open around the clock, employees frequently work varying shifts or variable schedules. Employees who work the late shift generally receive additional compensation. Many employees enjoy the opportunity to work part-time, nights or evenings, or other schedules that fit their availability for work and the hotel's needs. Hotel managers and many department supervisors may work regularly assigned schedules, but they also routinely work longer hours than scheduled, especially during peak travel times or when multiple events are scheduled. Also, they may be called in to work on short notice in the event of an emergency or to cover a position. Those who are self-employed, often owner-operators of small inns, camp sites, or RV parks, tend to work long hours and often live at the establishment or nearby.

Office and administrative support workers generally work scheduled hours in an office setting, meeting with guests, clients, and hotel staff. Their work can become hectic—processing orders and invoices, dealing with demanding guests, or servicing requests that require a quick turnaround. Job hazards typically are limited to muscle and eye strain common to working with computers and office equipment.

Computer specialists, information technology technicians, and audiovisual technicians who are employed mostly by larger convention hotels typically maintain standard hours servicing the property's Web sites and computer and communications networks. However, they often work long hours setting up and testing equipment for events that require their services.

Work in hotels and other accommodations can be demanding and hectic. Hotel staffs provide a variety of services to guests and must do so efficiently, courteously, and accurately. They must maintain a pleasant demeanor even during times of stress or when dealing with an impatient or irate guest. Alternately, work at slower times, such as the off-season or overnight periods, can seem slow and tiresome. Still, hotel workers must be ready to provide guests and visitors with gracious customer service at any hour.

Food preparation and food service workers in hotels must withstand the strain of working during busy periods and being on their feet for many hours. Kitchen workers lift heavy pots and kettles and work near hot ovens and grills. Job hazards include slips and falls, cuts, and burns, but injuries are seldom serious. Food service workers often carry heavy trays of food, dishes, and glassware. Many of these workers work part time, including evenings, weekends, and holidays.

Hotels and other accommodations provided 1.9 million wage and salary jobs in 2008. Employment is concentrated in cities and resort areas. Compared with establishments in other industries, hotels and other accommodations tend to be small. About 74 percent employed fewer than 20 workers and 54 percent employed fewer than 10. As a result, lodging establishments offer opportunities for those who are interested in owning or running their own business. Although establishments tend to be small, the majority of jobs are in larger hotels—those with more than 100 employees.

Hotels and other lodging places often provide first jobs to many new entrants to the labor force. In 2008, about 19 percent of the workers were younger than age 25, compared with about 13 percent across all industries.

The vast majority of workers in this industry—83 percent in 2008—were employed in service and office and administrative support occupations (table 1). Workers in these occupations usually learn their skills on the job. Postsecondary education is not required for most entry-level positions; however, college training may be helpful for advancement in some of the occupations. For those in administrative support—mainly hotel desk clerks—and service occupations, positive personality traits and a customer-service orientation may be more important than formal schooling. The most important traits for success in the hotels and other accommodations industry are good communication skills; the ability to get along with people in stressful situations; a neat, clean appearance; and a pleasant manner.

Service workers are by far the largest occupational group in the industry, accounting for 65 percent of the industry's employment. Most service jobs are in housekeeping occupations, including *maids and housekeeping cleaners* and *janitors and cleaners,* and in food preparation and serving jobs, including *waiters and waitresses, bartenders, fast food and counter workers,* and various other kitchen and dining room workers. The industry also employs many *baggage porters and bellhops, gaming services workers,* and *grounds maintenance workers.*

Workers in cleaning and housekeeping occupations ensure that the lodging facility is clean and in good condition for the comfort and safety of guests. *Maids and housekeeping cleaners* clean lobbies, halls, guestrooms, and bathrooms. They make sure that guests not only have clean rooms, but have all the necessary furnishings and supplies. They change sheets and towels, vacuum carpets, dust furniture, empty wastebaskets, and mop bathroom floors. In larger hotels, the housekeeping staff may include assistant housekeepers, floor supervisors, housekeepers, and executive housekeepers. *Janitors* help with the cleaning of the public areas of the facility, empty trash, and perform minor maintenance work.

Workers in the various *food preparation and serving* occupations deal with customers in the dining room or at a service counter. *Waiters and waitresses* take customers' orders, serve meals, and prepare checks. In smaller establishments, they often set tables, escort guests to their seats, accept payment, and clear tables. In larger restaurants, some of these tasks are assigned to other workers.

Hosts and hostesses welcome guests, show them to their tables, and give them menus. *Bartenders* fill beverage orders for customers seated at the bar or from waiters and waitresses who serve patrons at tables. *Dining room and cafeteria attendants* and *bartender helpers* assist waiters, waitresses, and bartenders by clearing, cleaning, and setting up tables, replenishing supplies at the bar, and keeping the serving areas stocked with linens, tableware, and other supplies. *Fast food and counter workers* take orders and serve food at fast-food counters and in coffee shops; they also may operate the cash register.

A variety of food preparation workers prepare food in the kitchen. Larger hotels employ *chefs and head cooks* who create menus, develop recipes, and oversee food preparation operations and personnel. *Food preparation and serving supervisors* direct workers and supervise specific tasks, such as overseeing banquet cooks or bartenders and servers at a private function, while the chef tends to other activities. *Restaurant cooks* specialize in the preparation of many different kinds of foods and menu items, generally cooking from scratch and typically only when ordered by diners. They may have titles such as salad chef, grill chef, or pastry chef. Individual chefs may oversee the day-to-day operations of different kitchens in a hotel, such as a full-service restaurant that specializes in fine-dining, a casual or counter-service establishment, or banquet operations.

Chef positions generally are attained after years of experience and, sometimes, formal training, including apprenticeships. Larger establishments also employ *executive chefs* and *food and beverage directors* who plan menus, purchase food, and supervise kitchen personnel for all of the kitchens in the property. *Food preparation workers* shred lettuce for salads, cut up food for cooking, and perform simple cooking steps under the direction of the chef or head cook. Beginners may advance to more skilled food preparation jobs with experience or specialized culinary training.

Many full-service hotels employ a uniformed staff to assist arriving and departing guests. *Baggage porters and bellhops* carry bags and escort guests to their rooms. *Concierges* arrange special or personal services for guests. They may take messages, arrange for babysitting, make restaurant reservations, provide directions, arrange for or give advice on entertainment and local attractions, and monitor requests for housekeeping and maintenance. *Doorkeepers* help guests into and out of their cars, summon taxis, and carry baggage into the hotel lobby.

Hotels also employ the largest percentage of *gaming services* workers because a large share of gaming takes place in casino hotels. Some gaming services positions are associated with oversight and direction—supervision, surveillance, and investigation—while others involve working with the games or patrons themselves, by tending the slot machines, handling money, writing and running tickets, dealing cards, and performing related duties.

The industry also employs a large number of *recreation and fitness workers*. At resort hotels and at vacation and recreational camps, recreation workers organize and conduct recreation activities for guests and campers. *Camp counselors* lead and instruct children and teenagers in outdoor-oriented forms of recreation, such as swimming, hiking, horseback riding, and camping. In addition, counselors at vacation and resident camps also provide guidance and supervise daily living and general socialization. Other types of campgrounds may employ trail guides for activities such as hiking, hunting, and fishing.

These positions accounted for 19 percent of the jobs in hotels and other accommodations in 2008. Hotel desk clerks, bookkeeping and accounting clerks, and switchboard operators ensure that the front office operates smoothly. *Hotel, motel, and resort desk clerks* process reservations and guests' registrations and checkouts, monitor arrivals and departures, handle complaints, and receive and forward mail. The duties of hotel desk clerks depend on the size of the facility. In smaller lodging places, one clerk or a manager may do everything. In larger hotels, a larger staff divides the duties among several types of clerks.

Hotels and other lodging places employ many different types of managers to direct and coordinate the activities of the front office, kitchen, dining room, and other departments, such as housekeeping, accounting, personnel, purchasing, publicity, sales, security, and maintenance. *Lodging managers*, typically the general manager and assistant managers, make decisions that affect the general operations of the hotel, including setting room rates, establishing credit policy, and having ultimate responsibility for resolving problems. In smaller establishments, lodging managers also may perform many of the front-office administrative tasks. In the smallest establishments, the owners—sometimes a family team—do all the work necessary to operate the business.

Other managers are responsible for different phases of hotel operations. For example, *food and beverage managers* oversee restaurants, lounges, and catering or banquet operations. *Rooms managers* look after reservations and occupancy levels to ensure proper room assignments and authorize discounts, special rates, or promotions. Large hotels, especially those with conference centers, use an executive committee structure to better facilitate departmental communications and coordinate activities. Other managers who may serve on a hotel's executive committee include *public relations* or *sales managers*, *human resource directors*, *executive housekeepers*, and *heads of hotel security*.

Most large hotel properties employ persons in occupations that require a wide range of skills and experience. Most entry-level jobs require little or no previous training; basic tasks usually can be learned in a short time. Lodging managers and many department heads usually require some formal training, or years of hospitality industry experience, or both. All positions in this industry require employees to maintain a customer-service orientation. Almost all workers in the hotel and other accommodations industry undergo some on-the-job training provided under the supervision of an experienced employee or manager to acclimate new employees to any unique characteristics of the property or the local area.

Hotel managers and owners recognize the importance of personal service and attention to guests, so they look for persons with positive personality traits and good communication skills when filling many guest services positions, such as desk clerk and host and hostess positions. Many hotel managers place a greater emphasis on customer service skills while providing specialized training in other skill areas, such as computer technology and software. Vocational courses and apprenticeship programs in food preparation, catering, and hotel and restaurant management, offered through restaurant and lodging associations and trade unions, provide training opportunities. Programs range in length from a few months to several years.

Service workers. Most service workers need only a high school diploma or equivalent to get hired, but some can be hired with even less. Some entry-level jobs are filled by students looking for part-time or seasonal work. Most hotels, particularly the chain hotels, have some formal training sessions for new employees that may include video or online training. Advancement opportunities for service workers in the hotel industry vary widely. Some workers, such as housekeepers and janitors, generally have few opportunities for advancement. In large properties, some may advance to supervisory positions. Advancement opportunities for chefs and cooks are better than those for most other service occupations. Cooks often advance to chef or to supervisory and management positions, such as executive chef, restaurant manager, or food service manager. Hotel desk clerks sometimes advance to supervisory or managerial front-office positions.

Promotional opportunities often are greatest for those who are willing to take on a new assignment in a different department. Advancement for those who excel at customer service and demonstrate a willingness to learn front-office jobs can serve as a steppingstone to jobs in public relations, advertising, sales, and management.

Management, business, and financial operations occupations. Many hotels fill first-level manager positions by promoting staff from within—particularly those with good communication skills, a solid educational background, tact, loyalty, and a capacity to endure hard work and long hours. People with these qualities still advance to manager jobs, but, more recently, lodging chains have primarily been hiring persons with 4-year college degrees in the liberal arts or other fields and starting them in assistant manager or management trainee positions. Bachelor's and Master's degree programs in hotel, restaurant, and hospitality management provide the strongest background for a career as a hotel manager, with nearly 150 colleges and universities offering such programs. Graduates of these programs are highly sought by employers in this industry because of their familiarity with technical issues and their ability to learn related skills quickly. Eventually, they may advance to a top management position in a hotel or a corporate management position in a large chain operation.

Upper management positions, such as general manager, food service manager, or sales manager, generally require considerable formal training and job experience. Some department managers, executive housekeepers, and executive chefs, generally require some specialized training and extensive on-the-job experience. To advance to positions with more responsibilities, lodging managers frequently change employers or relocate within a chain to a property in another area.

Office and administrative support occupations. For office and administrative support workers, advancement opportunities in the hotel industry vary widely. These occupations offer excellent entry-level job prospects and can serve as a steppingstone to jobs in hospitality, public relations, advertising, sales, and management.

The hotels and other accommodations industry is expected grow by 5 percent over the 2008-18 period. The industry employs large numbers of part-time and younger workers who typically do not stay in these jobs for very long. The need to replace these workers will create job opportunities in an array of occupations and localities.

Employment change. Wage and salary employment in hotels and other accommodations is expected to increase by 5 percent between 2008 and 2018, compared with 11 percent growth projected for all industries combined. Travel and tourism typically grows during expansion periods in the economy, which results in a greater need for transient rooms. The hotel market is expected to see increases in the number of rooms, but the greatest number of rooms is expected to open in limited service hotels that do not provide food service. Many of these newer hotels are being built in the suburbs where a growing population is increasingly based and a foundation of business establishments is being developed.

Employment outlook varies somewhat by service class of hotel and occupation. Growth of full-service hotels, casino hotels, and the smaller luxury hotel market that specializes in personal service will cause employment of lodging managers to grow more slowly than the average. The accelerating trend among chain-affiliated hotels to establish regional management and staffing teams among several properties and across service classes should provide current assistant managers or department managers with opportunities to demonstrate their readiness for advancement, but may also limit the prospects for new manager positions. Opportunities should be more limited for self-employed managers or owners of small lodging places, such as bed-and-breakfast inns, because of the competition from long-established chains as they move into untapped markets that were once friendly to the quainter properties. Job opportunities at outdoor recreation and RV parks should grow as RVs and driving vacations gain popularity in the United States. Also, gaming services and gaming manager occupations should grow as more casino hotels are built.

Employment of hotel, motel, and resort desk clerks is expected to grow faster than some other occupations in the industry in part because the growing numbers of limited-service hotels still require desk clerks. However, employment of dishwashers will decline within the industry—reflecting the increasing number of hotels and other accommodations that either do not offer full-service restaurants or contract them out to other food service establishments.

Job prospects. Although most of the hotels opening over the next decade will be limited-service hotels, most of the job openings will arise in full-service hotels, including convention, casino, and resort hotels, because they employ the most workers. Limited-service properties do not operate restaurants or lounges; therefore, these establishments offer a narrower range of employment opportunities. The streamlined organizational structure, however, offers a faster route to the general manager level for those more interested in running or owning their own hotel. Job opportunities will be concentrated in the largest hotel occupations, such as building cleaning workers and hotel, motel, and resort desk clerks. These workers are found in all types of hotels and accommodations, from the limited-service economy hotels to posh casino hotels. They also are important to the luxury hotel segment that emphasizes personal service.

Some occupations in this industry have relatively high numbers of workers who leave their jobs and must be replaced. Many young people, and those looking only for seasonal or part-time work, take food service and administrative jobs that require little or no previous training. To attract and retain workers, the hotel and other accommodations industry is placing greater emphasis on training and retaining employees. Job opportunities in this industry should be good for first-time jobseekers, people with limited experience, and those interested in making a career in the lodging industry.

Industry earnings. Earnings in hotels and other accommodations generally are much lower than the average for all industries. In 2008, average earnings for all nonsupervisory workers in this industry were $402 a week, compared with $608 a week for workers throughout private industry. Some workers in this industry earn the Federal minimum wage, which was $7.25 per hour as of July 2009. Some States have laws that establish a higher minimum wage.

Food and beverage service workers, as well as hosts and hostesses, maids and housekeeping cleaners, concierges, and baggage porters and bellhops, derive their earnings from a combination of hourly wages and customer tips. Waiters and waitresses often derive the majority of their earnings from tips, which vary greatly depending on menu prices and the volume of customers served. Many employers also provide free meals and furnish uniforms. Food service personnel may receive extra pay for working at banquets and on other special occasions. In general, workers with the greatest skills, such as restaurant cooks, have the highest wages, and workers who receive tips have the lowest. Wages in the largest occupations in hotels and other lodging places appear in table.

Median hourly wages of the largest occupations in hotels and other accommodations, May 2008

Occupation	Accommodations	All industries
Maintenance and repair workers, general	$12.47	$16.21
Cooks, restaurant	12.27	10.57
Janitors and cleaners, except maidsand housekeeping cleaners	10.76	10.31
Bartenders	9.55	8.54
Food servers, nonrestaurant	9.38	9.32
Hotel, motel, and resort desk clerks	9.34	9.37
Dining room and cafeteria attendants and bartender helpers	8.97	8.05
Waiters and waitresses	8.85	8.01
Maids and housekeeping cleaners	8.75	9.13
Gaming dealers	7.29	7.84

SOURCE: BLS Occupational Employment Statistics, May 2008.

Salaries of lodging managers are dependent upon the size and sales volume of the establishment and their specific duties and responsibilities. Managers may earn bonuses ranging up to 50 percent of their basic salary. In addition, they may be furnished with meals, parking, laundry, and other services, and sometimes on-site lodging for themselves and their families. Some hotels offer profit-sharing plans, tuition reimbursement, and other benefits to their employees.

About 8 percent of workers in hotels and other accommodations are union members or are covered by union contracts, compared with 14 percent of workers in all industries combined.

Performance Measurement

Performance measurement is the process whereby an organization establishes the parameters within which programs, investments, and acquisitions are reaching the desired results.

This process of measuring performance often requires the use of statistical evidence to determine progress toward specific defined organizational objectives. Fundamental purpose behind measures is to improve performance. Measures that are not directly connected to improving performance (like measures that are directed at communicating better with the public to build trust) are measures that are means to achieving that ultimate purpose (Behn 2003).

Behn 2003 gives eight reasons for adapting performance measurements:

1. **To Evaluate** how well a public agency is performing. To evaluate performance, managers need to determine what an agency is supposed to accomplish. (Kravchuk & Schack 1996). To formulate a clear, coherent mission, strategy, and objective. Then based on this information choose how you will measure those activities. (You first need to find out what are you looking for).

Evaluation processes consist of two variables: organizational performance data and a benchmark that creates a framework for analyzing that data. For organizational information, focus on the outcomes of the agency's performance, but also including input/ environment/ process/ output- to have a comparative framework for analysis. It is helpful to ask 4 essential questions in determining organizational data:

- Outcomes should be directly related to the public purpose of the organization. Effectiveness Q: did they produce required results (determined by outcomes).
- Cost-effective: efficiency Q (outcome divided by input).
- Impact Q: what value organisacion provides.
- Best-practice Q: evaluating internal operations (compare core process performance to most effective and efficient process in the industry).

As in order for organization to evaluate performance its requires standards (benchmark) to compare its actual performance against past performance/ from performance of similar agencies/ industry standard/political expectations.

2. **To Control** How can managers ensure their subordinates are doing the right thing.

Today managers do not control their workforce mechanically (measurement of time-and-motion for control as during Taylor) However managers still use measures to control, while allowing some space for freedom in the workforce. (Robert Kaplan & David Norton) Business has control bias. Because traditional measurement system sprung from finance function, the system has a control bias.

Organisation create measurement systems that specify particular actions they want execute- for branch employess to take a particular ways to execute what they want- branch to spend money. Then they want to measure to see whether the employees have in fact taken those actions. Need to measure input by individual into organisation and process. Officials need to measure behavior of individuals then compare this performance with requirements to check who has and has not complied.

Often such requirements are described only as guidelines. Do not be fooled. These guidelines are really requirements and those requirement are designed to control. The measurement of compliance with these requirements is the mechanism of control.

3. **To Budget** Budgets are crude tools in improving performance. Poor performance not always may change after applying budgets cuts as a disciplinary actions. Sometimes budgets increase could be the answer to improving performance. Like purchasing better technology because the current ones are outdated and harm operational processes. So decision highly influenced by circomstance, you need measures to better understand the situation.

At the macro level, elected officials deciding which purpose of government actions are primary or secondary. Political priorities drive macro budgetory choices. Once elected officials have established macro political priorities, those responsible for micro decisions may seek to invest their limited allocation of resources in the most cost-effective units and activities.

In allocating budgets, managers, in response to macro budget allocations (driven by political objectives), determin alloactions at the micro level by using measures of efficiency of various activities, which programs or organisations are more efficient at achieving the political objectives. Why spend limited funds on programs that do not guarantee exceptional performance?

Efficiency is determined by observing performance- output and outcome achieved considering number of people involved in the process (productivity per person) and cost-data (capturing direct cost as well as indirect)

4. **To Motivate** Giving people significant goals to achieve and then use performance measures- including interim targets- to focus people's thinking and work, and to provide periodic sense of accomplishment.

Performance targets may also encourage creativity in developing better ways to achieve the goal (Behn) Thus measure to motivate improvements may also motivate learning.

Almost-real-time output (faster, the better) compared with production targets. Quick response required to provide fast feed-back so workforce could improve and adapt.

Also it is able to provide how workforce currently performing.

Primary aim behind the measures should be output, managers can not motivate people to affect something over which they have little or no influence.

Once an agency's leaders have motivated significant improvements using output targets, they can create some outcomes targets.

- "output"- focuses on improving internal process.
- "outcome"- motivate people to look outside the agency (to seek way to collaborate with individuals & organisations may affect the outcome produced by the agency)

5. **To Celebrate** Organisations need to commemorate their accomplishments- such ritual tie their people together, give them a sense of their individual and collective relevance. More over, by achieving specific goals, people gain sense of personal accomplishment and selfworth (Locke & Latham 1984).

Links from measurement to celebration to improvement is indirect, because it has to work through one of the likes- motivation, learning...

Celebration helps to improve performance because it brings attention to the agency, and thus promotes its competence- it attracts resources.

- Dedicated people who want to work for successful agency.
- Potential collaborators.
- Learning-sharing between people about their accomplishments and how they achieved it.

Significant performance targets that provide sense of personal and collective accomplishement. Targets could ones used to motivate. In order for celebration to be a success and benefits to be a reality managers need to ensure that celebration creates motivation and thus improvements.

6. **To Promote** How can public managers convince political superiors, legislators, stakeholders, journalists, and citizens that their agency is doing a good job.

(National Academy of Public Administration's center for improving government performance- NAPA 1999) performance measures can be used to: validate success; justifing additional ressources; earn customers, stakeholder, and staff loyalty by showing results; and win recognition inside and outside the organisation.

Indirectly promote, competence and value of goverement in general.

To convince citizens their agency is doing good, managers need easily understood measures of those aspects of performance about which many citizens personally care.

("National Academy of Public Administration-NAPA" in its study of early performance- measurement plans under the government performance and results Act) most plans recognized the need to communicate performance evaluation results to higher level officials, but did not show clear recognition that the form and level of data for these needs would be different than that for operating managers. Different needs: Department head/ Executive Office of President/ Congress. NAPA suggested for those needs to be more explicitly defined- (Kaplan & Nortan 1994) stress that different customers have different concerns(1992).

7. **To Learn** Learning is involved with some process, of analysis information provided from evaluating corporate performance (identifying what works and what does not). By analysing that information, corporation able to learn resons behind its poor or good performance.

However if there is too many performance measures, managers might not be able to learn anything. (Neves of National Academy of Public Administration 1986)

- Because of rapid increase of performance measures there is more confusion or "noise" than useful data.

- Managers lack time or simply find it too difficult to try to identify good signals from mass of numbers.

Also there is an issue of "black box" enigma (data can reveal that organisation is performing well or poorly, but they don't necessarily reveal why). Performance measures can describe what is coming out of "black box" as well as what is going in, but they do not reveal what is happening inside. How are various inputs interacting to produce the output. What more complex is outcome with "black box" being all value chain.

Benchmarking is a traditional form of performance measurement which facilitates learning by providing assessment of organisational performance and identifying possible solutions for improvements.

Benchmarking can facilitate transfer of knowhow from benchmarked organisations. (Kouzmin et al. 1999)

Identifying core process in organisation and measuring their performance is basic to benchmarking. Those actions probably provide answer to issue presented in purpose section of the learning.

Measurements that are used for learning act as indicators for managers to consider analysis of performance in measurement's related areas by revealing irregularities and deviations from expected data results.

What to measure aiming at learning (the unexpected- what to aim for?)

Learning occurs when organisation meets problems in operations or failures. Then corporations improve by analysing those faults and looking for solutions. In public sector especially, failure usually punished severely- therefore corporations and individuals hide it.

8. **To Improve** What exactly should who- do differently to improve performance? In order for corporation to measure what it wants to improve it first need to identify what it will improve and develop processes to accomplish that.

Also you need to have a feedback loop to assess compliance with plans to achieve improvements and to determine if those processes created forecasted results (improvements).

Improvement process also related to learning process in identifying places that are need improvements.

Develop understanding of relationships inside the "black box" that connect changes in operations to changes in output and outcome.

Understanding "black box" processes and their interactions.

- How to influence/ control workforce that creates output.
- How to influence citizens/ customers that turn that output to outcome (and all related suppliers)

They need to observe how actions they can take will influence operations, environment, workforce and which eventually has an impact on outcome.

After that they need to identify actions they can take that will give them improvements they looking for and how organisation will react to those actions ex. How might various leadership activities ripple through the "black box".

Principles of Performance Measurement

All significant work activity must be measured.

- Work that is not measured or assessed cannot be managed because there is no objective information to determine its value. Therefore it is assumed that this work is inherently valuable regardless of its outcomes. The best that can be accomplished with this type of activity is to supervise a level of effort.
- Unmeasured work should be minimized or eliminated.
- Desired performance outcomes must be established for all measured work.
- Outcomes provide the basis for establishing accountability for results rather than just requiring a level of effort.
- Desired outcomes are necessary for work evaluation and meaningful performance appraisal.

- Defining performance in terms of desired results is how managers and supervisors make their work assignments operational.
- Performance reporting and variance analyses must be accomplished frequently.
- Frequent reporting enables timely corrective action.
- Timely corrective action is needed for effective management control.

If We Don't Measure

- How do you know where to improve?
- How do you know where to allocate or re-allocate money and people?
- How do you know how you compare with others?
- How do you know whether you are improving or declining?
- How do you know whether or which programs, methods, or employees are producing results that are cost effective and efficient?

Common problems with measurement systems that limit their usefulness:

- Heavy reliance on summary data that emphasizes averages and discounts outliers.
- Heavy reliance on historical patterns and reluctance to accept new structural changes (or re-design of processes) that are capable of generating different outcomes, like measuring the time it takes them to do a task.
- Heavy reliance on gross aggregates that tend to understate or ignore distributional contributions and consequences.
- Heavy reliance on static, e.g., equilibrium, analysis and slight attention to time-based and growth ones, such as value-added measures.

Performance Measurement Topics

Most of us have heard some version of the standard performance measurement cliches: "what gets measured gets done," " if you don't measure results, you can't tell success from failure and thus you can't claim or reward success or avoid unintentionally rewarding failure," " if you can't recognize success, you can't learn from it; if you can't recognize failure, you can't correct it," "if you can't measure it, you can neither manage it nor improve it," but what eludes many of us is the easy path to identifying truly strategic measurements without falling back on things that are easier to measure such as input, project or operational process measurements.

Performance Measurement is addressed in detail in Step Five of the Nine Steps to Success® methodology. In this step, Performance Measures are developed for each of the Strategic Objectives. Leading and lagging measures are identified, expected targets and thresholds are established, and baseline and benchmarking data is developed. The focus on Strategic Objectives, which should articulate exactly what the organization is trying to accomplish, is the key to identifying truly strategic measurements.

Strategic performance measures monitor the implementation and effectiveness of an organization's strategies, determine the gap between actual and targeted performance and determine organization effectiveness and operational efficiency.

Good Performance Measu

- Focus employees' attention on what matters most to success
- Allow measurement of accomplishments, not just of the work that is performed
- Provide a common language for communication
- Are explicitly defined in terms of owner, unit of measure, collection frequency, data quality, expected value(targets), and thresholds

- Are valid, to ensure measurement of the right things
- Are verifiable, to ensure data collection accuracy

Performance Measurement Systems

Several performance measurement systems are in use today, and each has its own group of supporters. For example, the Balanced Scorecard (Kaplan and Norton, 1993, 1996, 2001), Performance Prism (Neely, 2002), and the Cambridge Performance Measurement Process (Neely, 1996) are designed for business-wide implementation; and the approaches of the TPM Process (Jones and Schilling, 2000), 7-step TPM Process (Zigon, 1999), and Total Measurement Development Method (TMDM) (Tarkenton Productivity Group, 2000) are specific for team-based structures. With continued research efforts and the test of time, the best-of-breed theories that help organizations structure and implement its performance measurement system should emerge.

Although the Balanced Scorecard has become very popular, there is no single version of the model that has been universally accepted. The diversity and unique requirements of different enterprises suggest that no one-size-fits-all approach will ever do the job. Gamble, Strickland and Thompson (2007, p. 31) list ten financial objectives and nine strategic objectives involved with a balanced scorecard.

Problems in Performance Appraisals

- discourages teamwork
- evaluators are inconsistent or use different criteria and standards
- only valuable for very good or poor employees
- encourages employees to achieve short term goals
- managers has complete power over the employees
- too subjective
- produces emotional anguish

Solutions

- Make collaboration a criterion on which employees will be evaluated
- Provide training for managers; have the HR department look for patterns on appraisals that suggest bias or over or under evaluation
- Rate selectively(introduce different or various criteria and disclose better performance and coach for worst performer without disclosing the weakness of the candidate) or increase in frequency of performance evaluation.
- Include long term and short term goals in appraisal process
- Introduce M.B.O.(Management By Objectives)
- Make criteria specific and test selectively{Evaluate specific behaviors or results}
- Focus on behaviors; do not criticize employees; conduct appraisal on time.

5

Role of Supervisor in Hotel

In hotel industry, the main task of a supervisor is taking responsibility for customer satisfaction. This refers to the external customers as well as to the internal customers (service staff, kitchen) during the service hours. This does include being the active link between the management and the line staff.

Nevertheless, the definition is very vague and the position of the restaurant supervisor does include different responsibilities, depending on the environment and company.

Restaurant supervisors manage staff at all positions in a restaurant. Supervisors ensure that food preparation and customer service meet the standards of local regulatory agencies, the owners and management of the restaurant and the restaurant's patrons. Supervisors may also assist with other management tasks, such as scheduling and ordering supplies. Restaurant supervisors possess excellent people skills, strong organizational and leadership abilities and can work and troubleshoot in multiple areas of the restaurant.

MULTIPLE ROLE OF SUPERVISOR

Guest Service

Guest service is top priority in a restaurant. Supervisors assure that guests are being properly served and also resolve problems when they arise. Because the manner in which a problem is solved often determines whether a guest will return, good people skills and the ability to problem-solve are a priority for supervisors. They also create a welcoming atmosphere for restaurant patrons, greeting and saying goodbye to guests and stopping by tables to assure that all needs are being met.

Communication

Supervisors often act as a bridge between hourly staff and management. Supervisors communicate the roles, responsibilities and expectations of a job to employees and also pass along suggestions from staff about how to improve efficiency and guest service. As such, working as a restaurant supervisor requires strong communication skills.

Training

Supervisors assist management in training new employees as well as reviewing and reinforcing correct procedures and work habits for existing employees. For example, supervisors may hold staff meetings to inform servers of a new special or promotion. They may work with employees to improve their sales and guest service skills.

Compliance with Regulations

Many regulatory agencies govern restaurant operations, such as local health departments and the Department of Labor. Supervisors monitor and ensure compliance with applicable regulations. For example, restaurant supervisors confirm that staff members practice correct food-handling procedures, ensure that employees receive allotted breaks and enforce compliance with alcohol service laws.

Human Resources

Supervisors often act as the first point of contact when an employee has a problem. Supervisors relay concerns as needed to management and discipline or retrain employees who may not be performing to expectation. Supervisors may also conduct periodic performance reviews of staff and make recommendations for hiring, scheduling and promotion.

Sales and Reporting

Supervisors oversee sales, revenue and cash handling on their shift. They balance cash registers against reported sales and report any overages or shortages in money or inventory to management. Supervisors also complete reports on sales, labor and other costs on a daily basis, making organizational and computer skills assets of a skilled supervisor.

Other Duties

Supervisors should act as role models to hourly employees by helping as needed in the restaurant. Supervisors may work in all areas, from guest service to food preparation, and should possess a good working knowledge of cooking and handling food, as well as the ability to work efficiently in different positions and troubleshoot problems.

Ryugyong Hotel

The Ryugyong Hotel is a 105-floor skyscraper under construction in Pyongyang, North Korea. Its name comes from one of the historic names for the city of Pyongyang, and means "capital of willows";the building is also known as the 105 building, a reference to its number of floors. Construction began in 1987, but was halted in 1992 due to the economic disruptions that afflicted the country following the fall of the Soviet Union.

The hotel stood topped out but without windows or interior fittings for the next sixteen years. Construction resumed in April 2008, under the supervision of the Orascom Group of Egypt, which has invested heavily in the North Korean mobile telephony and construction industries.The company expected to complete exterior work on the building in 2010, with interior work taking until 2012 or later.

The hotel rises to a height of 330 metres (1,080 ft), and it contains 360,000 square metres (3,900,000 sq ft) of floor space, making it the most prominent feature of Pyongyang's skyline and by far the largest structure in North Korea. Construction of the Ryugyong was intended to be completed in time for the 13th World Festival of Youth and Students in June 1989; had this been achieved, it would have become the world's tallest hotel.

By total height the unfinished structure was not surpassed in height by another hotel until the completion of construction on the Rose Tower (Dubai, UAE) in 2009 due to its spire. But Ryugyong significantly higher than Rose Tower by height of roof and number of floors. Also, after a completion of Hotel tower of Abraj Al Bait Towers (Makkah, Saudi Arabia) even Ryugyong will be a hotel with maximum floors in world and one only with number of floors more than 100.

The Ryugyong is currently the world's 35-36th tallest building (a title it shares with the China World Trade Center Tower III) but by number of floors will became the 4th after completion and 9-10th later.

Historical Background

The plan for a large hotel was reportedly a Cold War response to the completion of the world's tallest hotel, the Westin Stamford Hotel in Singapore, in 1986 by a South Korean company, SsangYong Group. North Korean leadership envisioned the project as a channel for Western investors to step into the marketplace. A firm, the Ryugyong Hotel Investment and Management Co., was established to attract a hoped-for US$230 million in foreign investment.

A representative for the North Korean government promised relaxed oversight, saying, "The foreign investors can even operate casinos, nightclubs or Japanese lounges if they want to." North Korean construction firm Baikdoosan Architects & Engineers (also known as Baekdu Mountain Architects and Engineers) began construction on a pyramid-shaped hotel in 1987.

The hotel was scheduled to open in June 1989 for the 13th World Festival of Youth and Students, but problems with building methods and materials delayed completion. Had it opened on schedule, it would have surpassed the Westin Stamford Hotel to become the world's tallest hotel, and been ranked the seventh-tallest building in the world.

In 1992, after the building had reached its full architectural height,work was halted due to a lack of funds amid electricity and food shortages in North Korea.Japanese newspapers estimated the cost of construction was US$750 million, consuming 2 percent of North Korea's GDP. For over a decade, the unfinished building sat vacant and without windows, fixtures, or fittings, appearing as a massive concrete shell.A rusting construction crane at the top, which the BBC called "a reminder of the totalitarian state's thwarted ambition",became a permanent fixture.

In a 2006 article, ABC News questioned whether North Korea had sufficient raw materials or energy for such a massive project. A North Korean government official told the *Los Angeles Times* in 2008 that construction was not completed "because [North Korea] ran out of money".

Even though the Ryugyong dominates the Pyongyang skyline, official information regarding the hotel and its status have proven difficult to obtain. Though mocked-up images of the completed hotel had once appeared on North Korean stamps, the government denied the building's existence for many years, manipulated official photographs in order to remove the structure, and excluding it from printed maps of Pyongyang.

The alleged problems associated with the hotel led some media sources to dub it "The Worst Building in the World", "Hotel of Doom" and "Phantom Hotel".Former CNN international correspondent Mike Chinoy likened it to the calcium deposit on the neck of Kim Il-sung; both were clearly visible despite official attempts to hide them.

In April 2008, after 16 years of inactivity, work on the hotel was restarted by Egypt's Orascom Group. Orascom, which has entered into a US$ 400 million deal with the North Korean government to build and run a 3G mobile phone network, has denied that their telecommunications deal was directly related to the hotel work.

Features that Orascom has installed include exterior glass panels and telecommunications antennas. It is unclear to what extent Orascom plans to complete the building. In the late 1990s, the European Union Chamber of Commerce in Korea inspected the building and concluded that the structure was irreparable. Questions have been raised regarding the quality of the building's concrete and the alignment of its elevator shafts,which some sources say are "crooked".

In 2008, Orascom's resident project manager stated that, at a minimum, their goal was to make the facade more attractive.In 2009, Orascom's chief operating officer Khaled Bichara noted that, despite the reported structural problems of the building, interior work will be performed, and that a revolving restaurant will be located at the top of the building.

It is also unclear when the construction will be completed. In 2008, North Korean officials stated that the hotel would be completed by 2012, coinciding with the 100th anniversary of the birth of "Eternal President" Kim Il-sung. According to Orascom, work on the building's exterior is expected to last until the end of 2010, at which point interior work will begin, which will last until 2012 or beyond.

The Ryugyong is planned to become a mixed-use development, including "revolving restaurant" facilities along with "a mixture of hotel accommodation, apartments and business facilities" according to BBC quoting Orascom's Mr. Bichra.Other sources have hinted on the future multi-purpose nature of Ryugyong, including one quoting that Ryugyong's "3,000 rooms, offices, restaurants, nightclubs and banquet halls remain hollow shells."

Architecture

The Ryugyong Hotel consists of three wings, each measuring 100 metres (330 ft) long, 18 metres (59 ft) wide, and sloped at a 75-degree angle, which converge at a common point to form a pinnacle. The building is topped by a truncated cone 40 metres (130 ft) wide, consisting of eight floors that are intended to rotate, topped by a further six static floors. The structure was originally intended to house five revolving restaurants, and either 3,000 or 7,665 guest rooms, according to different sources.

Park Inn Hotel

Park Inn Hotel and City National Bank are two adjacent commercial buildings located in downtown Mason City, Iowa which were designed in the Prairie School style by the renowned architect Frank Lloyd Wright. Completed in 1910, the Park Inn Hotel is the last remaining Frank Lloyd Wright designed hotel in the world, of the six for which he was the architect of record.

The City National Bank is one of only two remaining Frank Lloyd Wright designed banks in the world. It was the first Frank Lloyd Wright designed project in the state of Iowa, and today carries both major architectural and historical significance. In 1999, the Park Inn Hotel was named on the Iowa Historic Preservation Alliance's Most Endangered Properties List.

Designated an official project of Save America's Treasures by the National Trust for Historic Preservation, the Park Inn Hotel is currently undergoing a complete renovation, including restoration of the distinctive brick and terra-cotta façade as well as art glass windows that will restore the Prairie School building to a functional boutique hotel by its centennial anniversary in 2010.

The Park Inn Hotel was the third hotel designed by Wright and served as the prototype for Midway Gardens in Chicago and the Imperial Hotel, Tokyo, which was torn down in 1962. In 1907, when law partners James E. Blythe and J. E. E. Markley were looking for an architect to compete in quality with the eight-story bank building that would be built across the corner, they didn't hesitate to give the commission to Frank Lloyd Wright, a young architect who was building a reputation in the Chicago area. For them Wright would build a complex, multi-purpose building that would give them multiple income streams.

Their law offices would be on the second floor of the building's narrower central waist and the hotel's east wing, surrounded on the south by a two-storey banking room with rental office space above. On the north would be a 42-room hotel, with basement shops beneath the Bank and Hotel. Wright managed to pack all these functions into an aesthetically well-integrated building that architecturally would be the bridge between Wright's Prairie School period and his Midway Gardens and the Imperial Hotel to follow.

Construction

Wright's drawings of the bank and hotel are dated from as early as December 17, 1908. Construction was begun on the first of April 1909, with supervision by Wright until his departure for Europe in late October of that year. At that time William Drummond from Wright's Oak Park Studio in Oak Park, Illinois took over the supervision of its construction and designed a nearby Prairie style home during his visits. The law office of developer-owners Blythe and Markley was open for business on August 29, 1910, with the gala opening of the entire structure September 10 of that year. Wright returned to the Midwest from his year in Europe in October 1910.

Unfortunately for the Park Inn Hotel, a new 250-room hotel with all the latest amenities was constructed in Mason City in 1922, creating stiff competition for the Park Inn Hotel. In addition, the farm crisis led to the closing of the City National Bank when was merged into another local bank. By 1925, four of the five banks in Mason City had failed.

In 1926, the City National Bank building was sold separately and underwent an unsympathetic remodeling into a new commercial use in that year. The upper floors of the Park Inn Hotel were eventually subdivided into rental apartments and over time the unique Prairie School design elements such as stained glass skylights, fixtures, furniture and woodwork were removed or lost. For the next several decades, the Park Inn experienced a gradual decline that ended with its closure in 1972.

Renovation

The Park Inn Hotel is currently undergoing a complete interior and exterior renovation thanks to numerous grants, as well as coordination at the local level. This includes a comprehensive restoration of the brick and terra-cotta façade, replacement of the art glass skylight windows, and a complete interior reconstruction.

Wright on the Park, Inc., the organization overseeing the work, has purchased the adjacent City Bank Building and with a plan to eventually reunite the Park Inn Hotel with the City National Bank. The group plans to refit the bank building with an elevator and provide six additional rooms for the hotel.

The restoration will be is on track for its reopening, in time for its centennial anniversary in 2010. This will build on Mason City's rich architectural heritage, which includes a history deep in Prairie School architecture from not just Wright, but many of his associates who built in Mason City, including Walter Burley Griffin, Marion Mahony Griffin, William Eugene Drummond and Francis Barry Byrne.

HOTEL MANAGEMENT IN SINGAPORE

Diverse Hotel Supervision Course in Singapore

There are a lot associated with hotel management courses in Singapore made available from well-well-known educational institutions with all the sole purpose of supplying students excellent understanding and means of development in order to be internationally competent in the food industry.

An example of which can be the Singapore Global Hotel and Travel and leisure College, an organization that is personal which offers half a dozen kinds of applications in culinary abilities, hotel management within Singapore, pastry as well as baking, tourism administration, hospitality management in addition to hotel and bistro operations.

Another is the particular Nanyang Polytechnic with a program that guides the students to a extensive, wide : based employment schooling using modules as well as hospitality and vacation business reviews, focusing in hotel supervision course in Singapore. Their students may have the chance to end up being potentially creative, reasonable thinkers, analytic orienied, swift in issue solving and have the expertise for good making decisions. Later in life, the scholars will find their particular niche in the steps of success since managers and professionals in the flourishing hotel, resorts and also tourism industries.

One more educational institution which usually is famous for it's quality education when it comes to hospitality is the University D' Hospitality. Being a member of the actual Shine Education Team, it primarily centers in hospitality schooling in congruence with all the Swiss hospitality that's widely established to make its students end up being fully equipped with the training and skills required to keep up with the actual changing times as well as maintains its best position on the international market especially in hotel management courses. It's located at the focus of Singapore and it is accessible to all kinds of transportation. As this is situated at Asia's crossroads, students will get to become involved in the lively and distinct social city. Also they are going to experience through the path of their learning use of international industries as well as have the chance to generate successful endeavors through other sides from the globe. The school is actually fully furnished significant materials and infrastructural units creating a breeding ground for students to understand.

The School D' Hospitality's record makes it be affiliates of the planet's famous institutions together with names like the Birmingham University, Sunderland School, UK's International Specialist Managers Association, Baltimore University in the United States associated with America and Beijing's Tsinghua University to mention only a few.

With all the highly competitive company in hospitality, the college D'Hospitality provides baccalaureate degrees and masteral programs in leisure time and tourism, gambling establishment management, hospitality administration and business government. With all these kinds of highlighted features of the institution, it is best to point out that through University D'Hospitality, students might be at par internationally considering that their own school has instituted in them any mindset of entrepreneurship and service frame of mind towards excellence.

Chef

A chef is a person who cooks professionally for other people. Although over time the term has come to describe any person who cooks for a living, traditionally it refers to a highly skilled professional who is proficient in all aspects of food preparation. The word "chef" is borrowed (and shortened) from the French term *chef de cuisine*, the director or head of a kitchen. (The French word comes from Latin *caput* and is cognate with English "chief".) In English, the title "chef" in the culinary profession originated in the *haute cuisine* of the 19th century. Today it is sometimes used to refer to any professional cook, regardless of rank.

Below are various titles given to those working in a professional kitchen and each can be considered a title for a type of chef. Many of the titles are based on the *brigade de cuisine* (or brigade system) documented by Auguste Escoffier, while others have a more general meaning depending on the individual kitchen. Not all restaurants will use these titles as each establishment may have its own set guidelines to organization. Specialized and hierarchal chef titles are usually found only in fine-dining, upscale restaurants; kitchen-staff members at casual restaurants such as diners are more often called "cook" or "short-order cook".

Chef de Cuisine, Executive Chef and H ead Chef

This person is in charge of all things related to the kitchen which usually includes menu creation; management, scheduling and payroll of entire kitchen staff; ordering; and plating design. *Chef de cuisine* is the traditional French term from which the English word chef is derived. *Head chef* is often used to designate someone with the same duties as an executive chef, but there is usually someone in charge of them, possibly making the larger executive decisions such as direction of menu, final authority in staff management decisions, etc. This is often the case for chefs with several restaurants.

Sous-chef

The *Sous-Chef de Cuisine* (under-chef of the kitchen) is the second in command and direct assistant of the Executive Chef. This person may be responsible for scheduling and substituting when the Executive Chef is off-duty and will also fill in for or assist the *Chef de Partie* (line cook) when needed. Smaller operations may not have a *sous-chef*, but larger operations may have several.

Expediter

The expediter (in French *aboyeur*) takes the orders from the dining room and relays them to the stations in the kitchen. This person also often puts the finishing touches on the dish before it goes to the dining room. In some operations this task may be done by either the executive chef or the *sous-chef*.

Chef de Partie

A *chef de partie*, also known as a "station chef" or "line cook",is in charge of a particular area of production. In large kitchens, each station chef might have several cooks and/or assistants. In most kitchens however, the station chef is the only worker in that department. Line cooks are often divided into a hierarchy of their own, starting with "first cook", then "second cook", and so on as needed.

Station-chef titles which are part of the brigade system include:

English	French	IPA	Description
sauté chef	*saucier*	[sosje]	Responsible for all sautéed items and their sauce. This is usually the highest stratified position of all the stations.
fish chef	*poissonnier*	[pwasoɲe]	Prepares fish dishes and often does all fish butchering as well as appropriate sauces. This station may be combined with the *saucier* position.
roast chef	*rôtisseur*	[ʁotisœʁ]	Prepares roasted and braised meats and their appropriate sauce.
grill chef	*grillardin*	[gʁijaʁdɛ̃]	Prepares all grilled foods; this position may be combined with the *rotisseur*.
fry chef	*friturier*	[fʁityʁje]	Prepares all fried items; this position may be combined with the *rotisseur* position.
vegetable chef	*entremetier*	[ɑ̃tʁəmetje]	Prepares hot appetizers and often prepares the soups, vegetables, pastas and starches. In a full brigade system a *potager* would prepare soups and a *legumier* would prepare vegetables.
roundsman	*tournant*	[tuʁnɑ̃]	Also referred to as a swing cook, fills in as needed on stations in the kitchen.
pantry chef	*garde manger*	[gaʁd mɑ̃ʒe]	Responsible for preparing cold foods, including salads, cold appetizers, *pâtés* and other *charcuterie* items.
butcher	*boucher*	[buʃe]	Butchers meats, poultry and sometimes fish. May also be responsible for breading meats and fish.
pastry chef	*pâtissier*	[patisje]	Prepares baked goods, pastries and desserts. In larger establishments, the pastry chef often supervises a separate team in their own kitchen or separate shop.

Commis

A commis is an apprentice in larger kitchens who works under a *chef de partie* to learn the station's responsibilities and operation. This may be a chef who has recently completed formal culinary training or is still undergoing training.

KITCHEN ASSISTANTS

Kitchen assistants (often known as kitchen porters or kitchenhands) are usually kitchen workers who assist with basic tasks, but have had no formal training in cooking. They carry out relatively unskilled tasks such as peeling potatoes and washing salad. In a smaller kitchen, assistants may be assigned a wider variety of tasks to reduce staffing costs.

A *communard* is in charge of preparing the meal for the staff during a shift. This meal is often referred to as the staff or family meal.

The *escuelerie* (from 15th century French and a cognate of the English "scullery") or dishwasher, is the keeper of dishes, having charge of dishes and keeping the kitchen clean. A common humorous title for this role in some modern kitchens is *chef de plúnge*or "Dish Pig".

United States and Canadian Training

Culinary education is available from a wide number of institutions offering diploma, associate, and bachelor degree programs in culinary arts. Depending on the level of education, this can take one to four years. An internship is often part of the curriculum. Regardless of the education received, most professional kitchens follow the apprenticeship system, and most new cooks will start at a lower-level *chef de partie* position and work their way up.

European Training

The training period for a chef is generally four years, consisting of first-year *commis*, second-year *commis*, and so on. The rate of pay is usually in accordance with the training status. *Commis* chefs are usually placed in sections of the kitchen (e.g., the starter (appetizer) or entrée sections) under the guidance of a *chef de partie* and are given relatively basic tasks. Ideally, over time, a *commis* will spend a certain period in each section of the kitchen to learn the basics. Unaided, a *commis* may work on the vegetable station of a kitchen.

The usual formal training period for a chef is two years in catering college. They often spend the summer in work placements. In some cases this is modified to 'day-release' courses; a chef will work full-time in a kitchen as an apprentice and then would attend catering college on days off. These courses can last between one to three years. Once the chef has completed the fourth year in training, they usually graduate to *demi-chef de partie* or *chef de partie*.

UNIFORM

The standard uniform for a chef includes a hat, necktie, double-breasted jacket, apron, houndstooth (check) trousers (to disguise stains) and shoes with steel or plastic toe-caps, or clogs. A chef's hat was originally designed as a tall rippled hat called a Dodin Bouffant. The Dodin Bouffant had 101 ripples that represent the 101 ways that the chef could prepare eggs. The modern chef's hat is tall to allow for the circulation of air above the head and also provides an outlet for heat. The hat helps to prevent sweat from dripping down the face. Skullcaps are an alternative hat worn by chefs.

Neckties were originally worn to allow for the mopping of sweat from the face, but as this is now against health regulations, they are largely decorative. The chef's neck tie was originally worn on the inside of the jacket to stop sweat running from face and neck down the body. The jacket is usually white to show off the chef's cleanliness and repel heat, and is double-breasted to prevent serious injuries from burns and scalds. The double breast also serves to conceal stains on the jacket as one side can be rebuttoned over the other.

An apron is worn to just below knee-length, also to assist in the prevention of burns because of spillage. If hot liquid is spilled onto it, the apron can be quickly removed to minimize burns and scalds. Shoes and clogs are hard-wearing and with a steel-top cap to prevent injury from falling objects or knives.

According to some hygiene regulations, jewelry is not allowed apart from wedding bands and religious jewelry. If wound dressings are required they should be blue—a colour not usual for foodstuffs—so that they are noticeable if they fall into food. Bandages on the hands are usually covered with rubber gloves.

ROOM SUPERVISOR JOB DESCRIPTION

A room supervisor offers hospitality in locker rooms, coatrooms or dressing rooms. He may provide personal items to customers, e.g., a room supervisor working in a public restroom offering patrons soap, lotions or towels. A room supervisor is also known as a locker room, coatroom or dressing room attendant.

A room supervisor's roles depends on her employer. However, all room supervisors deal with face-to-face customer service. According to the Occupational Information Network, room supervisors check supplies to make sure items are available. When necessary, she may order new supplies. Supplies for restroom or locker room supervisors may include towels, soaps, lotions and more. Room supervisors refer customer complaints or problems to management. She may also assign locker space, dressing room facilities or clothing containers to patrons of bathing or athletic establishments. She may answer customer inquires that include availability, policies, procedure or cost of facilities. Upon customer request, she may pick up food, beverages or other items. She also monitors guests and ensures they follow rules and regulations so that order and safety is maintained.

According to the U.S. Bureau of Labor Statistics Occupational Employment and Wages Survey Program, locker room, coatroom and dressing room attendants earn a median salary range of below $15,170 to above $31,050.

Amusement and recreation industries, golf courses and country clubs, skiing facilities, marinas, fitness and recreational sports centers and bowling centers all employ room supervisors. Other industries that employ high numbers of room attendants are traveler accommodation, personal care services, department stores and spectator sports.

Room supervisors may work in a fast-paced environment where customers quickly come and go, such as restrooms, whereas others may work in areas exclusive to a few guests, such as locker rooms in country clubs. A room supervisor may work part-time or full-time hours.

According to the BLS, locker room, coatroom and dressing attendants receive short-term on-the-job training from a manager or experienced room attendant. There are no official educational requirements, however, some establishments may require a high school diploma or its equivalent.

Housekeeping

Housekeeping is the act of cleaning the rooms and furnishings of a home. It is one of the many chores included in the term *housework*. Housecleaning includes activities such as disposing of rubbish, cleaning dirty surfaces, dusting and vacuuming. It may also involve some outdoor chores, such as removing leaves from rain gutters, washing windows and sweeping doormats. The term is often used also figuratively in politics and business, for the removal of unwanted personnel, methods or policies in an effort at reform or improvement.

Housecleaning is done to make the home look better and be safer and easier to live in. Without housecleaning limescale builds up on taps, mold grows in wet areas, bacterial action make the garbage disposal and toilet smell and cobwebs accumulate.Tools used in housecleaning include vacuum cleaners, brooms, mops and sponges, together with cleaning products such as detergents, disinfectants and bleach.

Disposal of rubbish is an important aspect of house cleaning, the reasons for this are psychological, social and practical. Plastic bags are designed and manufactured specifically for the collection of litter. Many are sized to fit common waste baskets and trash cans. Paper bags are made to carry aluminum cans, glass jars and other things. Recycling is possible with some kinds of litter.

Dusting

Over time dust accumulates on household surfaces. As well as making the surfaces dirty, when dust is disturbed it can become suspended in the air, causing sneezing and breathing trouble. It can also transfer from furniture to clothing, making it unclean. Various tools have been invented for dust removal;

Feather and lamb's wool dusters, cotton and polyester dust cloths, furniture spray , disposable paper "dust cloths", dust mops for smooth floors and vacuum cleaners. Vacuum cleaners often have a variety of tools to enable them to remove not just from carpets and rugs, but from hard surfaçes and upholstery.

Removal of Dirt

Examples of dirt or "soil" can be dry coffee spills and jelly drips or muddy footprints on carpet. Equipment used with a cleaner might be a bucket and sponge. A modern tool is the spray bottle, but the scientific principle is the same.

Household Chemicals

Various household cleaning products have been developed to facilitate the removal of dust and dirt, for surface maintenance, and for disinfection.Products are available in powder, liquid or spray form. The basic ingredients determine the type of cleaning tasks for which they are suitable. Some are packaged as general purpose cleaning materials whilst others are targeted at specific cleaning tasks such as drain clearing, oven cleaning, lime scale removal and polishing furniture.

Household cleaning products provide aesthetic and hygiene benefits but are also associated with health risks for the users, and building occupants.The US Department of Health and Human Services offers the public access to the Household Products Database. This database provides consumer information for over 4,000 products based on information provided by the manufacturer through the Material Safety Data Sheet.

Surfactants lower the surface tension of water, making it able to flow into smaller tiny cracks and crevices in soils making removal easier. Alkaline chemicals break down known soils such as grease and mud. Acids break down soils such as lime scale, soap scum, and stains of mustard, coffee, tea, and alcoholic beverages. Some solvent-based products are flammable and some can dissolve paint and varnish. Disinfectants stop smell and stains caused by bacteria.

When multiple chemicals are applied to the same surface without full removal of the earlier substance, the chemicals may interact. This interaction may result in a reduction of the efficiency of the chemicals applied (such as a change in pH value caused by mixing alkalis and acids) and in cases may even emit toxic fumes. An example of this is the mixing of ammonia-based cleaners (or acid-based cleaners) and bleach. This causes the production of chloramines that volatilize (become gaseous) causing acute inflammation of the lungs (toxic pneumonitis), long-term respiratory damage, and potential death.

Residue from cleaning products and cleaning activity (dusting, vacuuming, sweeping) have been shown to impact indoor air quality (IAQ) by redistributing particulate matter (dust, dirt, human skin cells, organic matter, animal dander, particles from combustion, fibers from insulation, pollen, and polycyclic aromatic hydrocarbons) that gaseous or liquid particles become adsorbed to.

The particulate matter and chemical residual will of be highest concentrations right after cleaning but will decrease over time depending upon levels of contaminants, air exchange rate, and other sources of chemical residual. Of most concern are the family of chemicals called VOCs such as formaldehyde, toluene, and limonene.

Volatile organic compounds (VOCs) are released from many household cleaning products such as disinfectants, polishes, floor waxes, air-freshening sprays, all purpose cleaning sprays, and glass cleaner. These products have been shown to emit irritating vapors. VOCs are of most concern due to their tendency to evaporate and be inhaled into the lungs or adsorbed to existing dust, which can also be inhaled.It has been found that aerosolized (spray) cleaning products are important risk factors and may aggravate symptoms of adult asthma, respiratory irritation,childhood asthma, wheeze, bronchitis, and allergy.

Other modes of exposure to potentially harmful household cleaning chemicals include absorption through the skin (dermis), accidental ingestion, and accidental splashing into the eyes. Products for the application and safe use of the chemicals are also available, such as nylon scrub sponge and rubber gloves. It is up to the consumer to keep themselves safe while using these chemicals. Reading and comprehending the labels is important.

There is a growing consumer and governmental interest in natural cleaning products and green cleaning methods. The use of nontoxic household chemicals is growing as consumers become more informed of the health effects of many household chemicals, and municipalities are having to deal with the expensive disposal of household hazardous waste (HHW).

Tools

"Modern housecleaning tools" is almost an oxymoron. There are few areas where someone from 50 years ago could step into the same job today, but housecleaning is an area where there has been very little change. Brooms remove debris from floors and dustpans carry dust and debris swept into them, buckets hold cleaning and rinsing solutions, vacuum cleaners and carpet sweepers remove surface dust and debris, chamois leather and squeegees are used for window-cleaning, and mops are used for washing floors.

A home's yard and exterior are sometimes subject to cleaning. Exterior cleaning also occurs for safety, upkeep and usefulness. It includes removal of paper litter and grass growing in sidewalk cracks. Rain gutters, doormats, pools and the screens and glass of windows are also cleanable. Yard junk-removal might occur and porch clutter removal. The paint of door frames might be washed or an old piñata thrown away.

WORK OF ROOM DIVISION MANAGERS

Room division managers are employed in hotels and lodges to oversee a team of booking clerks and front desk staff. Employed in a range of capacities from large resorts to small lodges, they ensure the reservation process runs smoothly and they deal with complaints and suggestions from guests. The Bureau of Labor Statistics (BLS) notes the industry is categorized by long hours, including evenings and weekends.

Most employers hire room division managers who have a bachelor's degree in business, hotel management or hospitality, according to the BLS. However, those who display leadership qualities and have gained experience in the hotel industry may be considered for trainee management roles. The BLS also notes that taking part in a formal internship is beneficial when trying to secure employment. In addition, a 2-year course called the "certified room division specialist" is also available in some high schools, which leads towards a post-secondary degree in hotel management.

A room division manager should have natural leadership qualities with the ability to give clear, concise instructions. Career Expo reports that room division managers should have a level of integrity, good manners and show initiative. The room division manager will be expected to deal with guest complaints and should therefore work well under pressure and keep calm in difficult situations.

The responsibilities of a room division manager vary depending on the size of the hotel or lodge and the number of managers employed. Typical day-to-day tasks of a room division manager will include overseeing the front desk members of staff including booking clerks and receptionists, coordinating reservations and monitoring room allocation, training and interviewing new members of staff, and dealing with customer complaints that have been escalated from more junior members of staff.

The salary range of a room division manager varies greatly depending on the size of hotel, level of management experience and geographical location. According to Indeed, the average annual salary of a room division manager in May 2008 was $43,000.

The BLS notes that seeking employment in hotels that offer the most guest services will face the toughest competition from others who are experienced in hotel management. Employment is predicted to grow by roughly 5 percent until 2018. The BLS reports hotel management roles often include long hours and at times can be stressful. College graduates with relevant work experience should enjoy the best employment opportunities, according to the BLS.

6

Training and Motivating Workers

Training quality service professionals is a task that gets better as time and experience with the practice progresses. A restaurant or hotel's level of service weighs heavily in the minds of patrons and is one of the key, deciding factors of returning business. In training staff, considerations such as education levels, hospitality industry experience and relative common sense all play roles in successfully training quality staff.

In the hospitality industry it is generally not required that potential candidates possess a number of degrees, nor is it necessary to have a staff that has ample experience in the field of hospitality. Chances are that hospitality staff members will come from diverse educational and professional backgrounds, and this factor can be quite useful. Important considerations in the hiring process of service professionals are personal appearance, the ability to communicate effectively with a wide range of people and the ability to grasp concepts quickly, as aspects of the service industry have a tendency to change rapidly. Ensuring that the proper candidates become an integral part of the service staff can make training a lot easier.

When training hospitality service staff it is important to impress upon new staff members the history of the company with whom they are employed. Service staff should be familiar with the mission of the company, established company standards and future operational goals. In teaching the history of the company new candidates are trained to think like a member of their new professional family, so to speak. Employees should be encouraged to share in the vision of the company and to thrive in accordance with the individual gifts they add to the professional community. Knowledge of the restaurant or hotel's history can also provide the new staff member with confidence in the place in which they work. This confidence can, in turn, be conveyed to the guest as a place where he can feel welcomed to enjoy his dining or lodging experience.

The cornerstone of most bars, restaurants and hotels are the food and beverage components of their businesses. When training new staff it is important to impress upon them the importance of having adequate food and beverage knowledge. On one hand, service staff must be able to describe and sell the various menu items to diners. Also, proper and readily available information saves service staff valuable time as having to retrieve information about menu items from someone else in the restaurant or hotel requires extra effort that may be needed elsewhere, especially during periods of high customer volume. A well-informed service professional instills confidence in the guest, both of the staff member and the establishment on the whole.

Many successful companies, as well as others that cannot quite tout this fact, fall short when it comes to providing overall quality customer service. The old adage, "don't judge a book by its cover" holds especially true when considering the abundance of restaurants and hotels available worldwide and the level of customer service these establishments provide. In training hospitality professionals it is highly important to teach the necessity of ensuring that customers either return to the business or would be inclined to recommend the establishment to a friend. Quite often, businesses possess the mentality of being more concerned about the guests they have at the moment instead of blending their concern with current and future guests. Teaching service professionals how to make a solid impression that will carry the dining experience into the future can be quite challenging but is the most rewarding to a business owner. Gestures of going the "extra mile," such as acknowledging each nearby guest with a greeting, making sure that glasses are never empty, offering information about local attractions and complimentary valet service can ensure that guests speak highly of their experience at your establishment.

IMPORTANCE OF TRAINING

In a hospitality setting, training simply means teaching people how to do their jobs. You may instruct and guide a trainee toward learning knowledge (such as certain facts and procedures), skills necessary to do the job to the standard required (such as loading the dishmachine), or attitudes (such as a guest-oriented attitude). Three kindsof training are needed in food and lodging operations:

1. Job instruction is just that, instruction in what to do and how to do it in every detail of a given job in a given enterprise. It begins on the first day and may be spread in small doses over several days, depending on how much needs to betaught and the complexity of the job.
2. Retraining applies to current employees. It is necessary when workers are not measuring up to standards, when a new method or menu or piece of equipment is introduced, or when a worker asks for it. It takes place whenever it is needed.
3. Orientation is the initial introduction to the job and the company. It sets the tone of what it is like to work for the company and explains the facility and the nitty-gritty of days and hours and rules and policies. It takes place before beginning work or in the first few days at work.

NEED FOR TRAINING

In our industry as a whole, we do very little of all three kinds of training. There is always that time pressure and that desperate need for someone to do the work right now, so we put untrained people to work and we hassle along with semicompetent or incompetent workers. Yet somehow we expect—or hope—that they will know how to do the work or can pick it up on the job, because we are not quite sure ourselves exactly what we want them to do.

The term training refers to the acquisition of knowledge, skills, and competencies as a result of the teaching of vocational or practical skills and knowledge that relate to specific useful competencies. It forms the core of apprenticeships and provides the backbone of content at institutes of technology (also known as technical colleges or polytechnics). In addition to the basic training required for a trade, occupation or profession, observers of the labor-market recognize today the need to continue training beyond initial qualifications: to maintain, upgrade and update skills throughout working life. People within many professions and occupations may refer to this sort of training as professional development.

Some commentators use a similar term for workplace learning to improve performance: training and development. One can generally categorize such training as *on-the-job* or *off-the-job*:

- On-the-job training takes place in a normal working situation, using the actual tools, equipment, documents or materials that trainees will use when fully trained. On-the-job training has a general reputation as most effective for vocational work.
- Off-the-job training takes place away from normal work situations — implying that the employee does not count as a directly productive worker while such training takes place. Off-the-job training has the advantage that it allows people to get away from work and concentrate more thoroughly on the training itself. This type of training has proven more effectivein inculcating concepts and ideas.

Training differs from exercise in that people may dabble in exercise as an occasional activity for fun. Training has specific goals of improving one's capability, capacity, and performance.

Physical Training

Physical training concentrates on mechanistic goals: training-programs in this area develop specific skills or muscles, often with a view to peaking at a particular time. Some physical training programs focus on raising overall physical fitness.

In military use, training means gaining the physical ability to perform and survive in combat, and learning the many skills needed in a time of war. These include how to use a variety of weapons, outdoor survival skills, and how to survive capture by the enemy, among others. See military education and training.

For psychological or physiological reasons, people who believe it may be beneficial to them can choose to practice relaxation training, or autogenic training, in an attempt to increase their ability to relax or deal with stress.While some studies have indicated relaxation training is useful for some medical conditions, autogenic training has limited results or has been the result of few studies.

Religion and Spirituality

In religious and spiritual use, training may refer to the purification of the mind, heart, understanding and actions to obtain a variety of spiritual goals such as (for example) closeness to God or freedom from suffering. Note for example the institutionalized spiritual training of Threefold Training in Buddhism, Yoga in Hinduism or discipleship in Christianity.

Compare religious and spiritual training with religious practice.

Artificial-intelligence Feedback

Researchers have developed training-methods for artificial-intelligence devices as well. Evolutionary algorithms, including genetic programming and other methods of machine learning, use a system of feedback based on "fitness functions" to allow computer programs to determine how well an entity performs a task. The methods construct a series of programs, known as a "population" of programs, and then automatically test them for "fitness", observing how well they perform the intended task. The system automatically generates new programs based on members of the population that perform the best. These new members replace programs that perform the worst.

The procedure repeats until the achievement of optimum performance.In robotics, such a system can continue to run in real-time after initial training, allowing robots to adapt to new situations and to changes in themselves, for example, due to wear or damage. Researchers have also developed robots that can appear to mimic simple human behavior as a starting point for training.

TRAINING SIMULATION

A training simulation is a virtual medium through which various different types of skills can be acquired. Training simulations can be used in a wide variety of genres; however they are most commonly used in corporate situations to improve business awareness and management skills. They are also common in academic environments as an integrated part of a business or management course.

The word simulation implies an imitation of a real-life process, usually via a computer or other technological device. This has proven to be a very reliable and successful method of training in thousands of industries worldwide.They can be used both to allow specialization in a certain area, and to educate individuals in the workings of the sectors as a whole, making training simulations incredibly versatile. It is important to emphasize that training simulations are not just games;their aim is to educate and inform in an exciting and memorable way, rather than purely to entertain.

Purpose

Companies across the world regularly use simulations as a tool to teach employees.With the enormous range of simulation-based activities available across the world, it is unsurprising that the specific aims of the sessions vary widely. Some simulations are focused on making decisions in a particular area of the business, such as personnel or product design, and these are called *Functional Simulations*. Others give a general overview of a company and give experience of making executive management decisions, and are called *Total Enterprise Simulations*.

In recent years, however, this classification has become somewhat impractical, as increasing numbers of training simulations are involving both elements, and combining both an overall view of the industry with some decisions relating to specific sectors.

Training Simulations normally form part of a programme designed to educate employees or students about the skills needed to operate a business, as well as persuade them to think outside the box and see the bigger picture.This can make for a better organized, more fluid system in which all employees understand their part in making the company successful.

FOR STUDENTS

Although the most common use for training simulations is in a corporate setting, simulation games are increasingly being used to educate young people about the importance of business. From secondary school age all the way up to MBA students, anyone can benefit from the first-hand experience of running a company and making decisions that directly affect performance. This will allow the participants to gain an overall understanding of the business world, and give some insight into the type of skills that are necessary to succeed.

It is also important to note that 'beating the game' should not be a primary aim for anyone taking part in a simulation; the focus should be directed towards everyone gaining some useful and relevant knowledge that they can take away and use in their daily lives. If the simulation does have a competitive element, it is to motivate and inspire, rather than encourage any malpractice.

Some training activities are non-competitive to avoid this, however many noted experts in the field state that the rivalry between teams or individuals improves the learning experience and adds a sense of fun and drama into the simulation. This is particularly important when working with young people such as students, as they often require an extra boost to keep them entertained, especially when a simulation is run over an extended period.

Development

The concept of training employees to have a wider perspective on their position within the workplace has been around for hundreds of years, but it is only relatively recently that the idea of creating a simulated environment for trainees to test their abilities and skills has been developed. The first commercially available training simulation was in 1956, and was called *The Top Management Decision Game,* and was created by the American Management Association. Since then, the market has expanded hugely, with thousands of simulations available based upon hundreds of different industries.

Initially very simple with just a few choices to make, some simulations have become extremely complex with many different interlinking decisions. When training simulations were first used, they involved paper forms that were filled in by the participants and then compared by the organizer of the exercise. Nowadays, nearly all simulations are computer based, and involve multi-stage algorithms that calculate performance based the decisions entered.

Most simulations are based around a real industry, and hence they use real data to be as accurate as possible and to provide a realistic experience. However, some remain generic and do not model a particular industry, although these tend to be more useful for younger players or those with absolutely no business knowledge.

Integrated Training Simulations

Most corporations and academic courses that contain a training simulation integrate it into an existing or completely new training programme. This allows the participants to get the maximum value from the experience, as well as review the sessions in order to improve them for future use. The structure of a training session would normally be as follows:

- **Introduction** - the organizer of the programme (plus sometimes a specialist in the training simulation) will meet the participants and give them a brief explanation of the purposes behind the training and what they should hope to achieve.
- **Lectures** - sometimes the trainees will also receive one or more lectures around the topics that the simulation will be based on, in order to give them an idea of the type of skills they will need. This is especially important within academia, when the students will often be examined on this section after the event.
- **The simulation** - the simulation will then be played, allowing newly-acquired knowledge to be tested and skills practiced. A positive atmosphere is vital here to maintain enthusiasm.
- **Evaluation** - once the simulation has been completed, it is very important to summarize what has been learnt and the effectiveness of the training. Presenting results to others may provide a means of internal assessment, as well as showcasing the players' achievements.

This integrated training will allow everyone taking part in the simulation to get the maximum experience possible, as well as being entertaining, exciting and giving them a new perspective on the business world. Many companies that specialize in training simulations also offer to create a special integrated plan unique to the client, to make the process as streamlined and efficient as possible.

Benefits

Since training simulations are available based on such a wide range of different industries, and with thousands of different aims and objectives, it is difficult to outline a specific skill-set that will be improved by taking part in a training simulation. However, skills that every good training simulation should build on include:

- **Business awareness** - before participating in the training programme, many players will have little idea of how to run a business or what it involves. Simulations allow them to temporarily have control over a virtual company, to see whether their decisions lead them to success or failure!
- **Time management and organization** - most simulations contain timed sessions, which will test the candidates' skill in submitting decisions within the allotted time slot. This is an excellent skill for any employee or graduate.
- **Team coordination** - the majority of training simulations involve working in groups or teams of people; improving the abilities to communicate effectively, delegate tasks and diplomatically resolve any situations.
- **Problem solving** - simulations will often present tricky circumstances that must be thought through logically to be solved. Successful resolution of these shows good management skills.

If every participant improves in these four key skill areas, the training programme will be a success, and any business should notice an improvement in efficiency and motivation, and students will be inspired and animated.

EXPERIENTIAL LEARNING

Experiential learning is the process of making meaning from direct experience. Aristotle once said, "For the things we have to learn before we can do them, we learn by doing them."David A. Kolb helped to popularize the idea of experiential learning drawing heavily on the work of John Dewey, Kurt Lewin, and Jean Piaget. His work on experiential learning has contributed greatly to expanding the philosophy of experiential education.

Experiential learning is learning through reflection on doing, which is often contrasted with rote or didactic learning. Experiential learning is related to, but not synonymous with, experiential education, action learning, adventure learning, free choice learning, cooperative learning, and service learning. While there are relationships and connections between all these theories of education, importantly they are also separate terms with separate meanings.

Experiential learning focuses on the learning process for the individual (unlike experiential education, which focuses on the transactive process between teacher and learner). An example of experiential learning is going to the zoo and learning through observation and interaction with the zoo environment, as opposed to reading about animals from a book. Thus, one makes discoveries and experiments with knowledge firsthand, instead of hearing or reading about others' experiences.

Experiential learning requires no teacher and relates solely to the meaning making process of the individual's direct experience. However, though the gaining of knowledge is an inherent process that occurs naturally, for a genuine learning experience to occur, there must exist certain elements. According to David Kolb, an American educational theorist, knowledge is continuously gained through both personal and environmental experiences. He states that in order to gain genuine knowledge from an experience, certain abilities are required:

1. the learner must be willing to be actively involved in the experience;
2. the learner must be able to reflect on the experience;
3. the learner must possess and use analytical skills to conceptualize the experience; and
4. the learner must possess decision making and problem solving skills in order to use the new ideas gained from the experience.

Effective Educational Method

Experiential learning can be a highly effective educational method. It engages the learner at a more personal level by addressing the needs and wants of the individual. Experiential learning requires qualities such as self-initiative and self-evaluation. For experiential learning to be truly effective, it should employ the whole learning wheel, from goal setting, to experimenting and observing, to reviewing, and finally action planning. This complete process allows one to learn new skills, new attitudes or even entirely new ways of thinking.

Most educators understand the important role experience plays in the learning process. A fun learning environment, with plenty of laughter and respect for the learner's abilities, also fosters an effective experiential learning environment. It is vital that the individual is encouraged to directly involve themselves in the experience, in order that they gain a better understanding of the new knowledge and retain the information for a longer time. As stated by the ancient Chinese philosopher, Confucius, "tell me and I will forget, show me and I may remember, involve me and I will understand."

According to learning consultants, experiential learning is about creating an experience where learning can be facilitated. How do you create a well-crafted learning experience? The key lies in the facilitator and how he or she facilitates the learning process. An excellent facilitator believes in the creed: "You teach some by what you say, teach more by what you do, but most of all, you teach most by who you are." And while it is the learner's experience that is most important to the learning process, it is also important not to forget the wealth of experience a good facilitator also brings to the situation.

An effective experiential facilitator is one who is passionate about his or her work and is able to immerse participants totally in the learning situation, allowing them to gain new knowledge from their peers and the environment created. These facilitators stimulate the imagination, keeping participants hooked on the experience.

Creating an experiential learning environment can be challenging for educators who have been taught through traditional classroom techniques. Identifying activities that allow learners to understand and absorb concepts can be a new and daunting experience. In traditional classrooms where lectures with PowerPoint slide sets are standard, educators need to be creative to engage students, get them up out of their chairs, involved in an experience. However, by providing direct experience in addition to standard written and visual materials, learners with different types of learning styles and strengths can be accommodated.

Sudbury model of democratic education schools assert that much of the learning going on in their schools, including values, justice, democracy, arts and crafts, professions, and frequently academic subjects, is done by learning through experience.

Comparisons

Experiential learning is most easily compared with academic learning, the process of acquiring information through the study of a subject without the necessity for direct experience. While the dimensions of experiential learning are analysis, initiative, and immersion, the dimensions of academic learning are constructive learning and reproductive learning. Though both methods aim at instilling new knowledge in the learner, academic learning does so through more abstract, classroom based techniques, whereas experiential learning actively involves the learner in a concrete experience.

Motivated Employees Ensure Success

No matter the size of your company, having a team of motivated, hard-working employees is crucial to your business success. When people lose their motivation, however, their job performance suffers — they become less productive, less creative, less of an asset to the company.

The bottom line: You pay a heavy price when employees have motivation issues.

How then to light a fire under an employee who has lost his or her motivation, whether a former hard worker whose performance has declined over the years, or a long-term problem employee who has failed to improve?

Here are 10 useful pointers on getting your employees enthused, productive, and ready to give their all:

1. **Build a foundation.** It's important to build a solid foundation for your employees so they feel invested in the company. Tell them about the history of the business and your vision for the future. Ask them about their expectations and career goals, as well as how you can help them feel part of the team. When any new employee starts, make sure he or she receives a thorough welcome orientation.
2. **Create a positive environment.** Promote an office atmosphere that makes all employees feel worthwhile and important. Don't play favorites with your staff. Keep office doors open and let folks know they can always approach you with questions or concerns. A happy office is a productive office.
3. **Put people on the right path.** Most employees are looking for advancement opportunities within their own company. Work with each of them to develop a career growth plan that takes into consideration both their current skills and future goals. If employees become excited about what's down the road, they will become more engaged in their present work.
4. **Educate the masses.** Help employees improve their professional skills by providing on-the-job training or in-house career development. Allow them to attend workshops and seminars related to the industry. Encourage them to attend adult education classes paid for by the company. Employees will feel you are investing in them, and this will translate into an improved job performance.
5. **Don't forget the fun.** Once in a while you have put work aside and do something nice for the people who work for you. Treat the office to a pizza lunch or take everyone to the movies. Reward employees with an unexpected day off or by closing the office early on a random Friday afternoon.

6. **Acknowledge contributions.** You can make a huge difference in employee morale simply by taking the time to recognize each employee's contributions and accomplishments, large or small. Be generous with praise.
7. **Provide incentives.** Offer people incentives to perform well, either with something small like a gift certificate or something more substantial such as a performance-based bonus or salary increase. Give out "Employee of the Month" awards. Such tokens of appreciation will go far in motivating employees.
8. **Honor your promises.** Getting people to give their all requires following through on promises. If you tell an employee that he or she will be considered for a bonus if numbers improve or productivity increases, you'd better put your money where your mouth is. Failure to follow through on promises will result in a loss of trust — not only that person's trust, but the trust of every employee that hears the story.
9. **Provide career coaching.** Help employees reach the next level professionally by providing on-site coaching. Bring in professionals to provide one-on-one counseling, which can help people learn how to overcome personal or professional obstacles on their career paths.
10. **Match tasks to talents.** You can improve employee motivation by improving employee confidence. Assign individuals with tasks you know they will enjoy or will be particularly good at. An employee who is successful at one thing will have the self-confidence to tackle other projects with renewed energy and excitement.

Motivating Your Work Force

If there's anything that's sunk lower than profit margins during the recession, it might be employee morale. And as workers get laid off, benefits get cut and stress takes hold, it's not just your associates who are suffering—guests are too, as they experience less than glowing service.

Fortunately for the hotel industry, there are ways to motivate your work force without breaking the bank, according to panelists during a breakout session at the Hotel Association of Canada's 2010 Annual Conference.

"Research tells us that professional development is usually at the top of the list of things that an employee values about their benefits in the workplace," said Wendy Swedlove, president of the Canadian Tourism Human Resource Council.

Other motivators include:

- a visible career path;
- a positive workplace atmosphere;
- flexibility (e.g. hours, benefits);
- a sense of employee empowerment; and
- compensation and benefits.

And while it's important to know the motivators, it's something else entirely to know how to implement them in a way that actually gets results. Here are four ways to motivate your work force during lean times:

1. Don't forget your managers—"How can you motivate folks if your managers aren't motivated?" asked Bill Pallett, senior VP of people resources and quality for Delta Hotels and Resorts, a management company with 44 properties throughout Canada.

"We as an industry go about this all wrong," he continued. "We're focusing on that front line, but we're forgetting that person who translates strategy into action on a daily basis."

While it's tempting to cut middle managers during lean times, Pallett strongly advised against doing so. Letting front-line associates clock-in without the supervision and coaching of a good manager is like setting passengers out to sea without an experienced captain.

Instead, remember your managers first in every morale-boosting initiative you set into action. If you make sure you motivate them, the rest will follow, Pallett said.

2. Communicate—There's nothing that breeds stress and anxiety like uncertainty, so it's imperative you keep the lines of communication open with employees, said Mo Aladin, director of operations for Cara Operations Limited, the largest operator of full-service restaurants in Canada.

The ways you enact that exchange of information can vary, from casual one-on-one discussions to companywide meetings. Aladin advised holding "state-of-the-union" gatherings to address any major changes within your company, as well as weekly updates within departments to keep everyone informed and up to speed.

While these updates invariably are easy to give when times are good, they're even more important when times are bad, he said. Therefore, you shouldn't be afraid to share bad news.

In one such instance, Aladin described how he went over the balance sheets for one restaurant location to justify to an employee why her hours were being cut. While she wasn't necessarily happy with the decision, taking the time to communicate with her made her much more accepting of the decision.

3. Set focused goals—Even when times are tough, you still can set focused goals to motivate your work force, the panelists agreed. One oft-cited example was improved guest satisfaction scores.

When doing so, just remember to measure your results and reward your employees for reaching their goals.

At Genesis Hospitality, for example, executive president Kevin Swark oversaw implementation of a points program that rewarded guests for improved performance. The company owns and operates six properties in Manitoba and Ontario.

"We have points for green ideas, staying healthy—if they don't use sick days—different things based on sales—if they sell so many bottles of wine or desserts," he said. " ... If they score a perfect mystery shop, they'll get points."

Employees then can use their accrued points in exchange for gift cards and other goods like iPods and golf clubs.

Swark admitted the program did require a significant investment on the part of the hotel owner and operator—to the tune of CAD$240,000 (US$233,806). But as employee and customer satisfaction scores increased, that upfront cost seemed more than worth it.

4. Train and train again—"Our biggest thing has been training, and training a lot more," Swark said.

While any training program requires some capital expenditure, they often yield the biggest returns of any motivational initiative. For one thing, professional development was cited as the most important thing employees value about their benefits in the workplace, according to a study conducted on behalf of the Canadian Tourism Human Resource Council.

Training programs show employees that you value their services, and that you're willing to put time and resources into making them better professionals.

That can go a long way in promoting employee loyalty, Swark said. At Genesis Hospitality, training initiatives helped reduce the company's turnover by half, saving tens of thousands of dollars, if not more.

Aladin said for every hourly worker that leaves, a company typically loses half that employee's salary on the bottom line. For management, it's even worse—a full year's salary.

Pallett agreed, saying that when figuring out the turnover's real cost, "that's a good rule of thumb."

But it's not just the cost that's a concern. How you treat your employees now will go a long way toward retaining them when the economy does turn around. And with historic work shortages predicted in Canada, that's an important consideration, the panelists agreed.

"People are going to remember how you treated them right now," Pallett said. "They don't forget. ... We need to be very cautious during this period of what might seem like a surplus (of workers)."

7

Team Building Always Works

Team building is an effort and does not happen naturally by its own. There are numerous great ideas for team building. We all know that working in a team can give strength to any organization, company or community. A good team can do wonders in any community or organization.

For good team building it is imperative to generate good ideas to balance the things involved. It is natural that initially the team members may have certain misconception and misunderstanding between them. But gradually this misunderstanding and misconception can be solved with effective team building steps.

No doubt conflict arises in any team but there is a solution to every problem There are numerous reasons involved in the conflict in a team and one of them is lack of trust. Lack of trust among the team members can create conflicts but can be solved with effective team building steps.

First of all, a good team requires a good team leader to lead. A good team leader should be a good source of motivation and encouragement. He should possess good leadership quality and the required aura around him. A team leader directs the team in proper channelized direction and removes the conflicts between the members.

Team leaders should also be capable of maintaining harmony and trust in the team. Proper focus and motivation should be provided by the team leader to the team. The team leader should always focus on the attainments of the objectives they are obliged to.

Generating Team Building Ideas—For those who are "born leaders" generating team building ideas is an easy task; but people who are given responsibility of handling the team based on their experience and skills can face some difficulty. Team building requires skills and dedication towards the members of the team. There are numerous team building ideas to resolve the problems and conflicts among the team members.

Team building ideas also helps to maintain balance and stability in the team. Proper presentation skills can also help you to maintain your team intact. You are able to convey your messages more clearly and precisely through good presentation skills.

Each and every team member should have clear understanding of the goals they are following. They should understand their available resources to reach their goals. They should also understand each other's responsibilities and limits. Team members should control their parts assigned to them.

They should also understand that they can give suggestion to their counterparts and not the orders except the juniors. Giving orders can sometimes lead to a conflict among the team members because of the ego and self respect involved.

Working in Group—It is always seen while working in a group that everyone wants the credit the work they have done. This creates a conflict. Team members should understand their responsibility and should work according to that.

Building trust should be another thing to build among the team members.

Members should be open to the meetings and discussions with their peers and colleagues. Open discussions and meetings will build a trust among the members. If all the problems and misunderstandings are solved then a thick layer of trust will form. It is also important to be loyal with your team members to build a certain amount of trust.

Try to socialize with the team members in order to build the understanding and the feeling of care. Socializing will also bring openness and interpersonal communication will get strengthen.

Active Participation—Try to allow each and every member to take part in the decision process. By this, the team members will feel that they are given a certain amount of importance and belongingness. This will automatically lead to their commitment to their goal. Team members should feel that they have contributed towards the goal, solution and on important decision made. The more they feel that they are important to the team the more they will be committed towards the team. This will lead to a good team building.

Always try to inform all team members about updates, about is happening in the team.. Team members should not feel that any of the important part is hidden from them. Always set a better communication line with the team members. Communication gap will again lead to a good amount of misunderstanding and can also hamper the goals undertaken.

Also remember to resolve the conflicts between the team members as soon as it rises up. Deal with the problems among the team members as soon as those problems come up. Do not give negative feedback to any of the team members. Negative feedback can hamper their work. Always try to give positive feedback with good notes. Try not to give any negative feedback in public places to the team members.

These are some great ideas for team building when applied effectively can do wonders to any organization or community. Try using them.

Team building refers to a wide range of activities, presented to businesses, schools, sports teams, religious or non-profit organizations designed for improving team performance. Team building is pursued via a variety of practices, and can range from simple bonding exercises to complex simulations and multi-day team building retreats designed to develop a team (including group assessment and group-dynamic games), usually falling somewhere in between.

It generally sits within the theory and practice of organizational development, but can also be applied to sports teams, school groups, and other contexts. Team building is not to be confused with "team recreation" that consists of activities for teams that are strictly recreational. Teambuilding is an important factor in any environment, its focus is to specialize in bringing out the best in a team to ensure self development, positive communication, leadership skills and the ability to work closely together as a team to problem solve.

Work environments tend to focus on individuals and personal goals, with reward & recognition singling out the achievements of individual employees. "How to create effective teams is a challenge in every organization"Team building can also refer to the process of selecting or creating a team from scratch.

Reasons for Team Building include :

- Improving communication
- Making the workplace more enjoyable
- Motivating a team
- Getting to know each other
- Getting everyone "onto the same page", including goal setting
- Teaching the team self-regulation strategies
- Helping participants to learn more about themselves (strengths and weaknesses)
- Identifying and utilizing the strengths of team members
- Improving team productivity
- Practicing effective collaboration with team members

TEAM BUILDING EXERCISES

Team building exercises consist of a variety of tasks designed to develop group members and their ability to work together effectively. There are many types of team building activities that range from kids games to games that involve novel complex tasks and are designed for specific needs.

There are also more complex team building exercises that are composed of multiple exercises such as ropes courses, corporate drumming and exercises that last over several days. The purpose of team building exercises is to assist teams in becoming cohesive units of individuals that can effectively work together to complete tasks.

Types of Team Building Exercises

Communication Exercise

This type of team building exercise is exactly what it sounds like. Communications exercises are problem solving activities that are geared towards improving communication skills. The issues teams encounter in these exercises are solved by communicating effectively with each other.

Goal: Create an activity which highlights the importance of good communication in team performance and/or potential problems with communication.

Problem Solving/Decision Making Exercise

Problem Solving/Decision making exercises focus specifically on groups working together to solve difficult problems or make complex decisions. These exercises are some of the most common as they appear to have the most direct link to what employers want their teams to be able to do.

Goal: Give team a problem in which the solution is not easily apparent or requires the team to come up with a creative solution

Planning/Adaptability Exercise

These exercises focus on aspects of planning and being adaptable to change. These are important things for teams to be able to do when they are assigned complex tasks or decisions.

Goal: Show the importance of planning before implementing a solution

Trust Exercise

A trust exercise involves engaging team members in a way that will induce trust between them. They are sometimes difficult exercises to implement as there are varying degrees of trust between individuals and varying degrees of individual comfort trusting others in general.

Goal: Create trust between team members

Subgroups of Team Building Exercises

- Simple social activities - to encourage team members to spend time together
- Group bonding sessions - company sponsored fun activities to get to know team members (sometimes intending also to inspire creativity)
- Personal development activities - individual programs given to groups (sometimes physically challenging)
- Team development activities - group-dynamic games designed to help individuals discover how they approach a problem, how the team works together, and discover better methods
- Psychological analysis of team roles, and training in how to work better together.

Team interaction involves "soft" interpersonal skills including communication, negotiation, leadership, and motivation - in contrast to technical skills directly involved with the job at hand. Depending on the type of team building, the novel tasks can encourage or specifically teach interpersonal team skills to increase team performance.

Models of Team Behavior

Team building generally sits within the theory and practice of organizational development. The related field of **team management** refers to techniques, processes and tools for organizing and coordinating a team towards a common goal - as well as the inhibitors to teamwork and ways to remove, mitigate or overcome them.

Several well-known approaches to team management have come out of academic work.

- The forming-storming-norming-performing model posits four stages of new team development to reach high performance. Some team activities are designed to speed up (or improve) this process in the safe team development environment.
- Belbin Team Types can be assessed to gain insight into an individual's natural behavioral tendencies in a team context, and can be used to create and develop better functioning teams.
- Team Sociomapping is an visual approach to team process and structure modelling. This model is based on social networks approach and improves the team performance by improvement of specific cooperation ties between the people.

Organizational Development

In the organizational development context, a team may embark on a process of self-assessment to gauge its effectiveness and improve its performance. To assess itself, a team seeks feedback from group members to find out both its current strengths and weakness.

To improve its current performance, feedback from the team assessment can be used to identify gaps between the desired state and the current state, and to design a gap-closure strategy. Team development can be the greater term containing this assessment and improvement actions, or as a component of organizational development.

Another way is to allow for personality assessment amongst the team members, so that they will have a better understanding of their working style, as well as their fellow team mates.

A structured teambuilding plan is a good tool to implement team bonding and thus, team awareness. These may De introduced by companies that does teambuilding sessionsm, or done internally by the human resource department.

A team-building consultant is responsible for each component of a team building intervention. He will likely interact with the team once, or for a limited number of times. During these first contacts, actively assessing the team, making recommendations, and providing activities (exercises that compose a team building intervention) for the team are the main responsibilities of the consultant. Moreover, usually a written proposal is required after the evaluation process, in which thc trainer indicates how he or she would go about improving the team's performance.

Once the organization and consultant determine which recommendations to utilize (if not all), the consultant is then responsible for providing a useful intervention that will transfer back into the organizational setting. This responsibility usually requires the consultant to create a detailed plan of events, while allowing for flexibility. After the intervention has been employed, the consultant will typically evaluate the team-building program and communicate the results to the organization.

Group Development

The goal of most research on group development is to learn why and how small groups change over time. To do this, researchers examine patterns of change and continuity in groups over time. Aspects of a group that might be studied include the quality of the output produced by a group, the type and frequency of its activities, its cohesiveness, the existence of conflict, etc.

A number of theoretical models have been developed to explain how certain groups change over time. Listed below are some of the most common models. In some cases, the type of group being considered influenced the model of group development proposed as in the case of therapy groups.

In general, some of these models view group change as regular movement through a series of "stages," while others view them as "phases" that groups may or may not go through and which might occur at different points of a group's history. Attention to group development over time has been one of the differentiating factors between the study of *ad hoc* groups and the study of teams such as those commonly used in the workplace, the military, sports and many other contexts.

In the early seventies, Hill and Grunner (1973) reported that more than 100 theories of group development existed. Since then, other theories have emerged as well as attempts at contrasting and synthesizing them. As a result, a number of typologies of group change theories have been proposed.

A typology advanced by George Smith (2001) based on the work of Mennecke and his colleagues (1992) classifies theories based on whether they perceive change to occur in a linear fashion, through cycles of activities, or through processes that combine both paths of change, or which are completely non-phasic.

Other typologies are based on whether the primary forces promoting change and stability in a group are internal or external to the group. A third framework advanced by Andrew Van de Ven and Marshall Scott Poole (1995), differentiates theories based on four distinct "motors" for generating change. According to this framework, the following four types of group development models exist:

Life cycle models: Describe the process of change as the unfolding of a prescribed and linear sequence of stages following a program that is prefigured at the beginning of the cycle (decided within the group or imposed on it).

Teleological models: Describe change as a purposeful movement toward one or more goals, with adjustments based on feedback from the environment.

Dialectical models: Describe change as emerging from conflict between opposing entities and eventual synthesis leading to the next cycle of conflict

Evolutionary models: Describe change as emerging from a repeated cycle of variation, selection and retention and generally apply to change in a population rather than change within an entity over time.

Some theories allow for combinations and interactions among these four "motors". For example, Poole (see below) found in his empirical research that seemingly complex patterns of behavior in group decision making result from the interplay of life-cycle and teleological motors.

An important observation made by McGrath and Tschan (2004) regarding the different models of group development found in the literature is that different models might explain different aspects of the history of a group. On the one hand, some models treat the group as an entity and describe its stages of development as a functioning unit or "intact system".

In this case, the models should be independent of the specific details of the task that the group is performing. On the other hand, some models might describe phases of the group's task performance and, because of this, tend to be very sensitive to the type of task that the group is engaged in (the "acting system", p. 101).

Below are descriptions of the central elements of some of the most common models of group development (See Smith, 2001 and Van de Ven & Poole, 1996 for a more complete list of theories and models).

Kurt Lewin's Individual Change Process

The first systematic study of group development was carried out by Kurt Lewin, who introduced the term "group dynamics" (Arrow et al., 2005). His ideas about mutual, cross-level influence and quasi-stationary equilibria, although uncommon in the traditional empirical research on group development, have resurged recently. His early model of individual change, which has served as the basis of many models of group development, described change as a three-stage process: unfreezing, change, and freezing.

Unfreezing: This phase involves overcoming inertia and dismantling the existing "mind set". Defense mechanisms have to be bypassed.

Change: In the second stage change occurs. This is typically a period of confusion and transition. One is aware that the old ways are being challenged but does not have a clear picture to replace them with yet.

Freezing: In the third stage the new mindset is crystallizing and one's comfort level is returning to previous levels. This is often misquoted as "refreezing" (see Lewin, 1947).

Tuckman's Stages Model

Bruce Tuckman reviewed about fifty studies of group development (including Bales' model) in the mid-sixties and synthesized their commonalities in one of the most frequently cited models of group development (Tuckman, 1965). The model describes four linear stages (forming, storming, norming, and performing) that a group will go through in its unitary sequence of decision making. A fifth stage (adjourning) was added in 1977 when a new set of studies were reviewed (Tuckman & Jensen, 1977).

Forming: Group members learn about each other and the task at hand. Indicators of this stage might include: Unclear objectives, Uninvolvement, Uncommitted members, Confusion, Low morale, Hidden feelings, Poor listening, etc.

Storming: As group members continue to work, they will engage each other in arguments about the structure of the group which often are significantly emotional and illustrate a struggle for status in the group. These activities mark the storming phase: Lack of cohesion, Subjectivity, Hidden agendas, Conflicts, Confrontation, Volatility, Resentment, anger, Inconsistency, Failure.

Norming: Group members establish implicit or explicit rules about how they will achieve their goal. They address the types of communication that will or will not help with the task. Indicators include: Questioning performance, Reviewing/

clarify objective, Changing/confirming roles, Opening risky issues, Assertiveness, Listening, Testing new ground, Identifying strengths and weaknesses.

Performing: Groups reach a conclusion and implement the solution to their issue. Indicators include: Creativity, Initiative, Flexibility, Open relationships, Pride, Concern for people, Learning, Confidence, High morale, Success, etc.

Adjourning: As the group project ends, the group disbands in the adjournment phase. This phase was added when Tuckman and Jensen's updated their original review of the literature in 1977.

Each of the five stages in the Forming-storming-norming-performing-adjourning model proposed by Tuckman involves two aspects: *interpersonal relationships* and *task behaviors*. Such a distinction is similar to Bales' (1950) equilibrium model which states that a group continuously divides its attention between instrumental (task-related) and expressive (socioemotional) needs.

As Gersick (1988) has pointed out, some later models followed similar sequential patterns. Examples include: define the situation, develop new skills, develop appropriate roles, carry out the work (Hare, 1976); orientation, dissatisfaction, resolution, production, termination (LaCoursiere, 1980); and generate plans, ideas, and goals; choose&agree on alternatives, goals, and policies; resolve conflicts and develop norms; perform action tasks and maintain cohesion (McGrath, 1984).

Tubbs' Systems Model

Stewart Tubbs "systems" approach to studying small group interaction led him to the creation of a four-phase model of group development:

Orientation: In this stage, group members get to know each other, they start to talk about the problem, and they examine the limitations and opportunities of the project.

Conflict: Conflict is a necessary part of a group's development. Conflict allows the group to evaluate ideas and it helps the group avoid conformity and groupthink

Consensus: Conflict ends in the consensus stage, when group members compromise, select ideas, and agree on alternatives.

Closure: In this stage, the final result is announced and group members reaffirm their support of the decision.

Fisher's Theory of Decision Emergence in Groups

Fisher outlines four phases through which task groups tend to proceed when engaged in decision making. By observing the distribution of act-response pairs (a.k.a. "interacts") across different moments of the group process, Fisher noted how the interaction changed as the group decision was formulated and solidified. His method pays special attention to the "content" dimension of interactions by classifying statements in terms of how they respond to a decision proposal (e.g. agreement, disagreement, etc.).

Orientation: During the orientation phase, group members get to know each other and they experience a primary tension: the awkward feeling people have before communication rules and expectations are established. Groups should take time to learn about each other and feel comfortable communicating around new people.

Conflict: The conflict phase is marked by secondary tension, or tension surrounding the task at hand. Group members will disagree with each other and debate ideas. Here conflict is viewed as positive, because it helps the group achieve positive results.

Emergence: In the emergence phase, the outcome of the group's task and its social structure become apparent. Group members soften their positions and undergo an attitudinal change that makes them less tenacious in defending their individual viewpoint.

Reinforcement: In this stage, group members bolster their final decision by using supportive verbal and nonverbal communication.

Based on this categorization, Fisher created his "Decision Proposal Coding System" that identifies act-response pairs associated with each decision-making phase. Interestingly, Fisher observed that the group decision making process tended to be more cyclical and, in some cases, almost erratic. He hypothesized that the interpersonal demands of discussion require "breaks" from task work.

In particular, Fisher observed that there are a number of contingencies that might explain some of the decision paths taken by some groups. For instance, in modifying proposals, groups tend to follow one of two patterns. If conflict is low, the group will reintroduce proposals in less abstract, more specific language. When conflict is higher, the group might not attempt to make a proposal more specific but, instead, because disagreement lies on the basic idea, the group introduces substitute proposals of the same level of abstraction as the original.

Poole's Multiple-sequences Model

Marshall Scott Poole's model suggests that different groups employ different sequences in making decisions. In contrast to unitary sequence models , the multiple sequences model addresses decision making as a function of several contingency variables: task structure, group composition, and conflict management strategies. Poole developed a descriptive system for studying multiple sequences, beyond the abstract action descriptions of previous studies.

From Bales' Interaction Process Analysis System and Fisher's Decision Proposal Coding System, Poole proposes 36 clusters of group activities for coding group interactions and 4 cluster-sets: proposal development, socioemotional concerns, conflict, and expressions of ambiguity. However, in his later work, Poole rejected phasic models of group development and proposed a model of continuously developing threads of activity. In essence, discussions are not characterized by blocks of phases, one after another, but by intertwining tracks of activity and interaction.

Poole suggests three activity tracks: task progress, relational, and topical focus. Interspersed with these are breakpoints, marking changes in the development of strands and links between them. Normal breakpoints pace the discussion with topic shifts and adjournments. Delays, another breakpoint, are holding patterns of recycling through information. Finally, disruptions break the discussion threads with conflict or task failure.

Task track: The task track concerns the process by which the group accomplishes its goals, such as dealing doing problem analysis, designing solutions, etc.

Relation track: The relation track deals with the interpersonal relationships between the group members. At times, the group may stop its work on the task and work instead on its relationships, share personal information or engage in joking.

Topic track: The topic track includes a series of issues or concerns the group have over time

Breakpoints: Breakpoints occur when a group switches from one track to another. Shifts in the conversation, adjournment, or postponement are examples of breakpoints.

McGrath's Time, Interaction, and Performance (TIP) Theory

McGrath's (1991) work emphasized the notion that different teams might follow different developmental paths to reach the same outcome. He also suggested that teams engage in four modes of group activity: *inception, technical problem solving, conflict resolution,* and *execution.*

According to this model, modes "are potential, not required, forms of activity" (p. 153) resulting in Modes I and IV (inception and execution) being involved in all group tasks and projects while Modes II (technical problem solving) and III (conflict resolution) may or may not be involved in any given group activity (Hare, 2003 uses the terms *meaning, resources, integration,* and *goal attainment* for these four modes).

McGrath further suggested that all team projects begin with Mode I (*goal choice*) and end with Mode IV (*goal attainment*) but that Modes II and III may or may not be needed depending on the task and the history of the group's activities. McGrath contended that for each identified function, groups can follow a variety of alternative "time-activity paths" in order to move from the initiation to the completion of a given function. Specifically, TIP theory states that there is a "default path" between two modes of activity which is "satisficing" or "least effort" path, and that such default path will "prevail unless conditions warrant some more complex path" (1991, p. 159).

Mode I: Inception Inception and acceptance of a project (goal choice)

Mode II: Technical Problem Solving: Solution of technical issues (means choice)

Mode III: Conflict Resolution : Resolution of conflict, that is, of political issues (policy choice)

Mode IV: Execution: Execution of the performance requirements of the project (goal attainment)

This model also states that groups adopt these four modes with respect to each of three team functions: *production, well-being,* and *member support*. In this sense, groups are seen as "always acting in one of the four modes with respect to each of the three functions, but they are not necessarily engaged in the same mode for all functions, nor are they necessarily engaged in the same mode for a given function on different projects that may be concurrent" (McGrath, 1991, p. 153). The following table illustrates the relationship between modes and functions.

Functions

	Production	**Well-being**	**Member Support**
Mode I: Inception	Production Demand/ Opportunity	Interaction Demand/ Opportunity	Inclusion Demand/ Opportunity
Mode II: Problem Solving	Technical Problem Solving	Role Network Definition	Position/ Status Attainment

	Production	Well-being	Member Support
Mode III: Conflict Resolution	Policy Conflict Resolution	Power/ Payoff Distribution	Contribution/ Payoff Relationships
Mode IV: Execution	Performance	Interaction	Participation

(Adapted from Figure 1 in McGrath, 1991, p. 154)

Gersick's Punctuated Equilibrium Model

Gersick's study of naturally occurring groups departs from the traditionally linear models of group development. Her punctuated equilibrium model (Gersick, 1988, 1989, 1991) suggests that groups develop through the sudden formation, maintenance, and sudden revision of a "framework for performance". This model describes the processes through which such frameworks are formed and revised and predicts both the timing of progress and when and how in their development groups are likely, or unlikely, to be influenced by their environments. The specific issues and activities that dominate groups' work are left unspecified in the model, since groups' historical paths are expected to vary. Her proposed model works in the following way.

Phase I : According to the model, a framework of behavioral patterns and assumptions through which a group approaches its project emerges in its first meeting, and the group stays with that framework through the first half of its life. Teams may show little visible progress during this time because members may be unable to perceive a use for the information they are generating until they revise the initial framework.

Midpoint : At their calendar midpoints, groups experience transitions-paradigmatic shifts in their approaches to their work-enabling them to capitalize on the gradual learning they have done and make significant advances. The transition is a powerful opportunity for a group to alter the course of its life midstream. But the transition must be used well, for once it is past a team is unlikely to alter its basic plans again.

Phase 2 : A second period of inertial movement, takes its direction from plans crystallized during the transition. At completion, when a team makes a final effort to satisfy outside expectations, it experiences the positive and negative consequences of past choices.

Wheelan's Integrated Model of Group Development

Building on Tuckman's model and based on her own empirical research as well as the foundational work of Wilfred Bion, Susan Wheelan proposed a "unified" or "integrated" model of group development (Wheelan, 1990; Wheelan, 1994a). This model, although linear in a sense, takes the perspective that groups achieve maturity as they continue to work together rather than simply go through stages of activity. In this model "early" stages of group development are associated with specific issues and patterns of talk such as those related to dependency, counter-dependency, and trust which precede the actual work conducted during the "more mature" stages of a group's life. The table below describes each one of these phases.

Stage I Dependency and Inclusion: The first stage of group development is characterized by significant member dependency on the designated leader, concerns about safety, and inclusion issues. In this stage, members rely on the leader and powerful group members to provide direction. Team members may engage in what has been called "pseudo-work," such as exchanging stories about outside activities or other topics that are not relevant to group goals.

Stage II Counterdependency and Fight: In the second stage of group development members disagree among themselves about group goals and procedures. Conflict is an inevitable part of this process. The group's task at Stage 2 is to develop a unified set of goals, values, and operational procedures, and this task inevitably generates some conflict. Conflict also is necessary for the establishment of trust and a climate in which members feel free to disagree with each other.

Stage III Trust / Structure: If the group manages to work through the inevitable conflicts of Stage 2, member trust, commitment to the group, and willingness to cooperate increase. Communication becomes more open and task-oriented. This third stage of group development, referred to as the trust and structure stage, is characterized by more mature negotiations about roles, organization, and procedures. It is also a time in which members work to solidify positive working relationships with each other

Stage IV Work / Productivity: As its name implies, the fourth stage of group development is a time of intense team productivity and effectiveness. Having resolved many of the issues of the previous stages, the group can focus most of its energy on goal achievement and task accomplishment

Final: Groups that have a distinct ending point experience a fifth stage. Impending termination may cause disruption and conflict in some groups. In other groups, separation issues are addressed, and members' appreciation of each other and the group experience may be expressed.

Based on this model, Wheelan has created and validated both a *Group Development Observation System* (GDOS) and a *Group Development Questionnaire* (GDQ). The GDOS allows researchers to determine the developmental stage of a group by categorizing and counting each complete thought exhibited during a group session into one of eight categories: *Dependency* statements, *Counterdependency, Fight, Flight, Pairing, Counterpairing, Work,* or *Unscorable* statements (Wheelan, 1994). The GDQ is used to survey group members and assess their individual perception of their group's developmental state (Wheelan, S., & Hochberger, 1996). Her academic work has been transferred into a commercial organization, GDQ Associates, Inc.

In her empirical validation of the model, Wheelan (2003) has analyzed the relationship between the length of time that a group has been meeting and the verbal behavior patterns of its members as well as the member's perceptions of the state of development of the group. Her results seem to indicate that there is a significant relationship between the length of time that a group had been meeting and the verbal behavior patterns of its members.

Also, members of older groups tended to perceive their groups to have more of the characteristics of Stage-3 and Stage-4 groups and to be more productive. Based on these results, Wheelan's position supports the traditional linear models of group development and casts doubt on the cyclic models and Gersick's punctuated equilibrium model.

Morgan, Salas & Glickman's TEAM Model

Combining multiple theories and the development models of Tuckman and Gersick, Morgan, Salas and Glickman (1994) created the Team Evolution and Maturation (TEAM) model to describe a series of nine developmental stages through which newly formed, task-oriented teams are hypothesized to evolve. The periods of development are labeled "stages" and conceived to be "relatively informal, indistinct, and overlapping", because "sharp demarcations are not often characteristic of the dynamic situations in which operational teams work and develop".

According to this model, teams might begin a given period of development at different stages and spend different amounts of time in the various stages. Teams are not always expected to progress in a linear fashion through all of the stages. A team's beginning point and pattern of progression through the stages depend on factors such as the characteristics of the team and team members, their past histories and experience, the nature of their tasks, and the environmental demands and constraints (cf. McGrath, 1991).

The Team model identities a total of *nine stages*, seven central ones supplemented by two additional ones. The seven central stages begin with the formation of the team during its first meeting (forming) and moves through the members' initial, and sometimes unstable, exploration of the situation (storming), initial efforts toward accommodation and the formation and acceptance of roles (norming), performance leading toward occasional inefficient patterns of performance (performing-I), re-evaluation and transition (reforming), refocusing of efforts to produce effective performance (performing-11), and completion of team assignments (conforming).

The development of a team might be recycled from any of the final stages to an earlier stage if necessitated by a failure to achieve satisfactory performance or if adjustments to environmental demands are required or if problematic team interactions develop.

The core stages of the model are preceded by a pre-forming stage that recognizes the forces from the environment (environmental demands and constraints) that call for, and contribute to, the establishment of the team; that is, forces external to the team (before it comes into existence) that cause the team to be formed. The last stage indicates that after the team has served its purpose, it will eventually be disbanded or de-formed. Here. individuals exit from the group (separately or simultaneously) and the team loses its identity and ceases to exist.

The TEAM model also postulates the existence of *two distinguishable activity tracks* present throughout all the stages. The first of these tracks involves activities that are tied to the specific task(s) being performed. These activities include interactions of the team members with tools and machines, the technical aspects of the job (e.g., procedures, policies, etc.), and other task-related activities. The other track of activities is devoted to enhancing the quality of the interactions, interdependencies, relationships, affects, cooperation, and coordination of teams.

The proponents of the model did not test its components or sequence of stages empirically but did confirm that the perceptions of team members concerning the performance processes of the team are perceived to include both team-centered and task-centered activities and that these perceptions seem to change over time as a result of team training.

If you're like most people, the mere mention of the term "teambuilding" probably sends a shiver up your spine, bringing to mind past episodes of self-conscious camaraderie among co-workers at a medieval theme restaurant or being forced to fall awkwardly backwards into the arms of a fellow employee.

It's true that teambuilding can be uncomfortable. However, recent research confirms that by working through these obstacles together, personnel can overcome their surface-level differences and develop a more profound sense of mutual trust, respect, and cooperation. Not coincidentally, these qualities also happen to be defining characteristics of teams that are equipped to deliver the kind of top-quality customer service that is necessary for long-term success in the highly competitive hospitality industry.

EFFECTIVE TEAMBUILDING IN THE HOSPITALITY INDUSTRY

Experts and researchers agree that properly administered teambuilding initiatives can foster positive outcomes ranging from increased morale to improved profits. In the specific context of the hospitality industry, most studies have evaluated the ability of teambuilding exercises to impact turnover, a persistent problem that has long plagued the hospitality labor market.

Again and again, research data have shown that effective teambuilding programs can dramatically increase the rate of retention among hospitality workers. However, ineffectively administered teambuilding efforts may have the opposite effect of pushing staff members so far out of their comfort zones that they become alienated and disinvested from the organization.

Effective teambuilding exercises have also been shown to foster improved communication, cooperation, and solidarity among managers and staff members. In the hospitality industry, these variables can promote a dynamic, interdependent working environment and organizational culture that can generate truly exceptional customer service.

Because service quality is such a singularly important factor in determining the success level of a particular property or brand, organizations seeking to maintain a strong competitive position in the hospitality industry should explore the potential promise of teambuilding exercises.

Meaningless Amusements

Some critics have derided the current trend of teambuilding exercises as little more than meaningless amusements that are unlikely to prompt meaningful changes within a company's organizational culture. However, a number of notable studies have linked ongoing teambuilding exercises with improvements in team functioning, cooperation, and communication, as well as increased retention.

Still, the criticism of some stand-alone teambuilding efforts does have a measure of validity. Not every group activity that staff members engage in should be regarded as teambuilding. Sometimes, an outing should be scheduled that is intended purely as entertainment or reward to deepen the sense of camaraderie among team members.

Teambuilding Initiative

A major inadequacy of many teambuilding efforts is the failure to link the exercises to concerns, problems, or challenges that exist within the organization. In order to maximize the return on investment of the time, effort, and resources that will be invested in the teambuilding program, it is important to make as many tacit and explicit connections as possible between the organization's real-world challenges and the learning exercise.

Encourage Organization-wide Participation

One of the most common mistakes that organizations make when planning teambuilding activities is focusing solely on staff-level employees. However, in order to foster true teambuilding, experts recommend that a cross-section of the company should be represented, ranging from executives to support staff. Clear interest and dedication from the upper-tier managers and decision-makers will greatly augment the kind of connections, trust, and morale that are the goals of teambuilding exercises.

Introduce the Lessons Learned into Workplace

Before, during, and after the teambuilding exercise, it is crucial to maintain a dialogue about the significance and meaning of the activity. A 15-20 minute open discussion period after the conclusion of the activity should be planned to help the employees process what they've learned, and periodic follow-ups can reinforce the lessons in the long-term.

Develop a Long-term Teambuilding Plan

In some cases, a single, stand-along teambuilding exercise can be sufficient to spark a major change in the culture of a workplace. However, the best results are often gained through an extended teambuilding initiative. The incremental accumulation of lessons learned through teambuilding over a sustained period of time is most likely to foster deep-seated change in the organization.

Some Suggested Teambuilding Activities

According to Karen Clark Frederick, proprietor of Teambuilding Adventures in Birmingham, Michigan, some ideas for effective teambuilding activities include ropes courses, team sports, outdoor excursions, obstacle courses, military exercises, skill-based competitions, charitable campaigns, volunteer work, drum circles, scavenger hunts, art projects, paintball excursions, game tournaments, retreats.

RESEARCH METHODS

Apart from the question of the validity of the research methods used and the generalizations that can be made based on the types of groups studied, there still remain some significant challenges in the study of group development. As some researchers have pointed out group development models often provide only snapshots of groups at certain points of their history but do not fully describe the mechanisms of change, the "triggers" that lead to change or the amount of time that a group might remain in a stage. Furthermore, naturally occurring groups tend to be highly sensitive to outside influences and environmental contingencies, but few models account for these influences.

Models of "small" group development are also related to those of organization development but operate at a different level of analysis. Despite their differences, both areas of work attempt to understand patterns and processes of collective change. Both fields should strive to develop "process-oriented" theories, which according to Poole and Van de Ven (2004):

- Provide a deep understanding of how change comes about by describing the generative mechanism that drives the process;
- Can account for path dependence and the role of critical events in change and innovation; and
- Can incorporate the role of human agency in change without reducing it to causal terms.

A number of questions still remain unanswered in the study of group development over time. As McGrath and Tschan (2004) stated, some of these challenges include:

- Do groups of all types change in the same way?
- Are the temporal patterns in groups in fact developmental stages with the changes patterned so that the same kinds of structures and processes occur in the same fixed sequences for all groups?
- If there is a fixed sequence of stages of development, are the stages of equal or different durations? Do all groups go through these stages at the same rate?
- Is the pattern of stages immutable or subject to alteration by unique circumstances or events external to the group?
- If a given group does not follow a fixed sequence of stages, is variation in the sequence indicative of malfunction in the group's development or maturation, or does it merely express normal variation arising from initial or contextual conditions?

8

Developing Employee Schedules

Managers and owners in the Hospitality industry face enormous obstacles every time they sit down to schedule staff for the multiple positions that must be filled every night. Consisting of broad category of fields within the service industry that includes lodging, restaurants, event planning, theme parks, transportation, cruise line, and additional fields within the tourism industry, Hospitality deals with high employee turnover and demanding clientele. As any manager in this industry knows, there is little to no margin for error when it comes down to scheduling.

Shift Planning will help Hospitality Industry employees have a say in their own shift schedules, and improve the efficiency for managers who are responsible for making sure the right manpower is in the right place, at the right time.

No matter what size or type of Hospitality industry business you own or manage, the unique demands placed on your scheduling needs calls for a powerful online tool designed to streamline the process of hiring, managing, scheduling and communicating with all of your company's staff.

Shift Planning is a complete employee scheduling and labor management solution for the businesses that fall in the Hospitality industry, providing one-click seamless access to time and attendance, employee scheduling, and management reports. Managers using Shift Planning spend more time managing, and less time stuck in an office juggling schedules and labor expenses.

EFFECTIVE WORKPLACE SCHEDULE

A **schedule**, often called a rota, is a list of employees who are working on any given day, week, or month in a workplace. A schedule is necessary for the day-to-day operation of any retail store or manufacturing facility. The process of creating a schedule is called scheduling. An effective workplace schedule balances the needs of employees, tasks, and in some cases, customers. A *daily* schedule is usually ordered chronologically, which means the first employees working that day are listed at the top, followed by the employee who comes in next, *et cetera*.

A *weekly* or *monthly* schedule is usually ordered alphabetically, employees being listed on the left hand side of a grid, with the days of the week on the top of the grid. A schedule is most often created by a manager. In larger operations, a Human Resources manager or scheduling specialist may be solely dedicated to writing the schedule.

A schedule by this definition is sometimes referred to as workflow. In some cases, scheduling software is used to allow organizations to better manage staff scheduling. Employee scheduling software supports shift and employee assignments and improves staff utilization.Organizations commonly use spreadsheet software or employee scheduling software to create and manage shifts, assignments, and employee preferences. Advanced employee scheduling software also provides ways to connect with the staff, ask for their preferences and communicate the schedule to them, via email or SMS.

EMPLOYEE SCHEDULING SOFTWARE

Employee scheduling software automates the process of creating and maintaining a schedule. Such software will usually track vacation time, sick time, compensation time, and alert when there are conflicts. As a database of schedules are accumulated over time, it may analyze past activity and prepare data for payroll. Although it may not make strategic decisions to lower costs and improve performance, it does manage the tasks.

For smaller businesses it is increasingly important to keep the costs low on this administrative task, which can be quite large keeping the composition of the modern workforce in mind. Many smaller businesses have part time workers who may be studying on the side or have other jobs they attend to. Flexible management of availability of the employees, shift trading, automatic scheduling processes and such are key in keeping the costs down. Many vendors are based exclusively online to meet the increasingly web savvy workforce of today.

Scheduling is also done in aviation for flying crews i.e. cockpit crews and cabin crews. Scheduling software enables generation of schedules for the crew on a weekly or monthly basis, providing schedules on the basis of guidelines provided by Civil Aviation requirements, which differ from country to country. These requirements also change when a carrier flies internationally or crosses borders. This software may be a part of an ERP package or a module of such packages, which is effective for an operations department.

Benefits

Employee scheduling software can be an essential part of everyday business processes. Although software won't improve business practices by itself, it does automate typically tedious business administration. Some even calculate factors such as approved employee requests, hours of availability, business hours, business needs, shift trades, etc; and automatically create a work schedule that fits everybody's needs.

Shift scheduling experts can be hired to work on strategic challenges if your team can't go it alone, but software typically manages the task of automation and data collection. By providing large amounts of data, management teams can use that data to form opinions and create actionable plans. Some of the benefits are listed below:

- Better achievement of contracted service level agreements
- Field workers completing more jobs per day
- Improved worker, equipment and vehicle utilization
- Increases transparency of field operations
- Minimized job administration costs

Small businesses should consider a variety of factors when evaluating software or web based staff scheduling solutions:

- Learning curve - how quickly staff will be able to get up and running with the new solution.
- Ability to maintain the schedule - web based solutions provide a high level of availability versus locally installed solutions.
- Ability to let staff members collaborate on the schedule - provide their preferences and swap shifts between them.
- Ability to easily identify unassigned shifts.
- Ability to create reports for invoicing and payroll.

Shift work

Shift work is an employment practice designed to make use of the 24 hours of the clock. The term "shift work" includes both long-term night shifts and work schedules in which employees change or rotate shifts.. A related yet different concept, the work shift, is the time period during which a person is at work.

A day may be divided into three shifts, each of 8 hours, and each employee works just one of those shifts; they might, for example, be midnight to 08:00, 08:00 to 16:00, 16:00 to midnight. Generally, "first shift" refers to the day shift, with "second shift" running from late afternoon to midnight or so, and "third shift" being the night shift. On occasion, more complex schedules are used, sometimes involving employees changing shifts, in order to operate during weekends as well, in which case there will be four or more sets of employees.

12-hour work shifts are also in use. In a modern steelworks, four sets of personnel are used, working consecutive days in one 12-hour shift (06:00 – 18:00 and vice-versa). Shift A will work days, and shift B nights, over a 48-hour period, before handing over to shifts C and D and taking 48 hours off. In the offshore petroleum industry, employees may work 14 consecutive days or nights, 06:00 – 18:00 or 18:00 – 06:00, followed by three or four weeks free. The *svingskift* (literally: "swing shift") in the offshore petroleum industry in Norway refers to a two-week tour during which employees work 12-hour days the first seven days and 12-hour nights the second (or vice versa).

Shift work was once characteristic primarily of the manufacturing industry, where it has a clear effect of increasing the use that can be made of capital equipment and allows for up to three times the production compared to just a day shift. It contrasts with the use of overtime to increase production at the margin. Both approaches incur higher wage costs.

Although 2nd-shift worker efficiency levels are typically 3–5% below 1st shift, and 3rd shift 4–6% below 2nd shift, the productivity level, i.e. cost per employee, is often 25% to 40% lower on 2nd and 3rd shifts due to fixed costs which are "paid" by the first shift.

In general, requiring workers to live on a time-shifted schedule for extended periods is unpopular, and this typically must be paid for at a premium. It is common in heavy industry, particularly automobile and textile manufacturing and is becoming more common in locations where a shut-down of equipment would incur an extensive restart process. Food manufacturing plants, in particular, have extensive cleaning programs that are required before any restart.

The use of shift work in manufacturing varies greatly from country to country. Shift work has been traditional in law enforcement and the armed forces: for example sailors must be available to handle a vessel around the clock, and a system of naval watches organized to ensure enough hands are on duty at any time. This is shift work by another name.

Service industries now increasingly operate on some shift system; for example a restaurant or convenience store will normally each day be open for much longer than a working day. Shift work is also the norm in governmental and private employment in fields related to public safety and healthcare, such as police, fire prevention, security, emergency medical transportation and hospitals. Companies working in the field of meteorology, such as the National Weather Service and private forecasting companies, also utilize shift work, as constant monitoring of the weather is necessary.

Much of the Internet services industry relies on shift work to maintain worldwide operations and uptime.

Shift Patterns

Three-shift System

The "three-shift system" is the most common pattern, with "first" from 06:00 to 14:00, "second" from 14:00 to 22:00, and a "third" (or "night") shift from 22:00 to 06:00 This is generally worked over a five-day week; to provide coverage 24/7, employees have their days off ("weekends") on different days.

All of the shifts have desirable and less desirable qualities. First shift has very early starts, so time in the evening before is heavily cut short. The second shift (or "swing shift") occupies the times during which many people finish work and socialize. The third shift creates a situation in which the employee must sleep during the day.

Generally, employees stay with the same shift for a period of time, as opposed to cycling through them; this is seen as healthier.

Three-shift example:

Time	Sat	Sun	Mon	Tues	Wed	Thur	Fri
06:00–14:00	**Shift 1**	**Shift 1**	**Shift 1**	**Shift 1**	**Shift 1**	Off	Off
14:00–22:00	**Shift 2**	**Shift 2**	**Shift 2**	**Shift 2**	**Shift 2**	Off	Off
22:00–06:00	**Shift 3**	**Shift 3**	**Shift 3**	**Shift 3**	**Shift 3**	Off	Off

Four on, Four off

Four on, four off is a shift pattern that is being heavily adopted in the United Kingdom and in some parts of the United States. An employee works for four days, usually in 12-hour shifts (7:00 to 7:00) then has four days off. While this creates a "48-hour week"(42-hour average over the year) with long shifts, it may be preferred because it shrinks the work week down to four days, and then gives the employee four days rest—double the time of a usual weekend.

Due to the pattern, employees effectively work an eight-day week, and the days they work vary by "week". As with three-shift system, most employees stay with the same shift rather than cycling through them.

Four on, four off example:

Time 7:00-7:00	Sat	Sun	Mon	Tues	Wed	Thur	Fri	Sat
07:00–19:00	Day 1	Off	Off	Day 4	Off	Off	Off	Off
19:00–07:00	Off	Day 2	Day 3	Off	Off	Off	Off	Off

Four on, Three off

Each employee works four days and gets a three-day weekend. For some types of manufacturing, this is a win-win arrangement. For example, Kyanize Paint Company had been making 3 batches of paint per day, Monday through Friday (3 × 5 = 15). They changed to making 4 batches of paint, Monday through Thursday (4 × 4 = 16). Total worker hours remained the same, but profits increased. In exchange for two additional hours of work per day, over 4 days, workers got an additional day off every week (see also the book, 4 Days, 40 Hours).

Four on, Two off

In *four on, two off* the employee only gets two days off. In a seven-day period, this adds up to 60 hours worked (on average, based on 12-hour shifts). Four on, two off is mainly adopted by industries in which employees do not engage in much physical activity.

Four on, two off example:

Time	Sat	Sun	Mon	Tues	Wed	Thur	Fri
07:00 to 19:00	Day 1	Day 2	Day 3	Day 4	Off	Off	Day 5

Four on, One off

In *four on, one off* the employee only gets one day off. In a seven-day period, this adds up to 48 hours worked (on average, based on 8-hour shifts). Four on, one off is mainly adopted by industries in which companies prefers to work for all days of the week with four shifts and where laws do not let employees work for 12 hours a day for several days.

Four on, one off example:

Time	Sat	Sun	Mon	Tues	Wed	Thur	Fri
07:00–15:00	Day 1	Day 2	Day 3	Day 4	Off	Day 5	Day 6

Two Days, Two Nights, Four off

A variation is the *two days, two nights, four off* pattern of working. In this shift schedule, employees work 12-hour shifts from 06:00 to 18:00 on day shifts and from 18:00 to 06:00 on nights. This pattern is currently in use by HM Coastguard in the UK, and employs four separate teams to maintain 24/7 coverage.

Two days, two nights, four off example:

Time	Sat	Sun	Mon	Tues	Wed	Thur	Fri	Sat
06:00–18:00	Day 1	Day 2	Off	Off	Off	Off	Off	Off
18:00–06:00	Off	Off	Day 3	Day 4	Off	Off	Off	Off

5/4/9s

"5/4/9s" (or "Five/Four Nines") is another variation. Employees work in 2 week cycles. Week 1 the employee works 4 days of 9 hours followed by 1 day of 8 hours with 2 days off (week 1: 44 hours). Week 2 the employee works 4 days of 9 hours with 3 days off (week 2: 36 hours). This pattern works to 80-hours in a 2 week pay-period (comparable to working 8 hours a day for 5 days a week).

The benefit to working an extra hour a day gives you a "normal" 2 day weekend followed by a long 3 day weekend the next. Typical working hours for this type of shift would be 06:00 to 15:30 (9 hours with 30 minutes lunch) and 06:00 to 14:30 (8 hours with 30 minutes lunch) on the 8-hour work day. Often the employer will alter the starting times (e.g., start at 07:00 or 08:00). Also referred to as "9/80" as employees have nine days to work 80 hours.

5/4/9s shift example:

Week	Mon	Tues	Wed	Thur	Fri	Sat	Sun
Week 1	9 hrs	9 hrs	9 hrs	9 hrs	8 hrs	Off	Off
Week 2	9 hrs	9 hrs	9 hrs	9 hrs	Off	Off	Off

12/24/12/48

12/24/12/48 (or *12/24*) is another variation. Employees work in shifts of 12 hours; first a daily shift (e.g., 07:00 to 19:00), followed by 24 hours rest, then a nightly shift (19:00 to 07:00), finishing with 48 hours rest. This pattern needs four teams for full coverage, and makes an average 42-hour workweek.

12/24/12/48 shift example:

Time	Sat	Sun	Mon	Tues	Wed	Thur	Fri
07:00–19:00	Day 1	Off	Off	Off	Day 3	Off	Off
19:00 to 07:00	Off	Day 2	Off	Off	Off	Day 4	Off

Continental Shift

Continental shift, adopted primarily in central Europe, is a rapidly changing three-shift system that is usually worked for seven days straight, after which employees are given time off. For example, three mornings, two afternoons, and then two nights.

Continental shift example:

Time	Sat	Sun	Mon	Tues	Wed	Thur	Fri
06:00–14:00	Shift 1	Shift 1	Shift 1	Off	Off	Off	Off
14:00 to 22:00	Off	Off	Off	Shift 1	Shift 1	Off	Off
22:00–06:00	Off	Off	Off	Off	Off	Shift 1	Shift 1

Split Shift

Split shift is used primarily in the catering, transport, hotel, and hospitality industry. Waiters and chefs work for four hours in the morning (to serve lunch), then four hours in the evening (to serve an evening meal). The average working day of a chef on split shifts could be 10:00 to 14:00 and then 17:00 to 21:00

Split shift example:

Time	Sat	Sun	Mon	Tues	Wed	Thur	Fri
10:00–14:00	On	On	On	On	On	Off	Off
14:00–17:00	Off	Off	Off	Off	Off	Off	Off
17:00–21:00	On	On	On	On	On	Off	Off

Earlies and Lates

Earlies and lates is used primarily in industries such as customer service (help desk/phone-support), convenience stores, child care (day nurseries), and other businesses that require coverage greater than the average 9:00 to 5:00 working day in the UK. Employees work in two shifts that largely overlap, such as *early shift* from 08:00 to 16:00 and *late shift* from 10:00 to 18:00

Earlies and lates shift example:

Time	Sat	Sun	Mon	Tues	Wed	Thur	Fri
08:00–16:00	Shift 1	Shift 1	Shift 1	Shift 1	Shift 1	Off	Off
15:00–23:00	Shift 2	Shift 2	Shift 2	Shift 2	Shift 2	Off	Off

7-day Fortnight Shift

In the *7-day fortnight shift* pattern, employees work their allotted hours within 7 days rather than 10. Therefore, 41 hours per week equate to 82 hours per fortnight (fourteen days and nights), which is worked in seven days, at 11–12 hours per shift. This shift structure is used in the broadcast television industry, as well as many law enforcement agencies in the US.

7-day fortnight shift example:

Week 1

Time	Sat	Sun	Mon	Tues	Wed	Thur	Fri
Days 08:00 to 20:00	Shift 'A' Day 1	Shift 'A' Day 2	Shift 'C' Day 1	Shift 'C' Day 2	Shift 'C' Day 3	Shift 'A' Day 3	Shift 'A' Day 4
Nights 20:00 to 08:00	Shift 'B' Night 1	Shift 'B' Night 2	Shift 'D' Night 1	Shift 'D' Night 2	Shift 'D' Night 3	Shift 'B' Night 3	Shift 'B' Night 4

Week 2

Time	Sat	Sun	Mon	Tues	Wed	Thur	Fri
Days 08:00 to 20:00	Shift 'C' Day 4	Shift 'C 'Day 5	Shift 'A' Day 5	Shift 'A' Day 6	Shift 'A' Day 7	Shift 'C' Day 6	Shift 'C' Day 7
Nights 20:00 to 08:00	Shift 'D' Night 4	Shift 'D' Night 5	Shift 'B' Night 5	Shift 'B' Night 6	Shift 'B' Night 7	Shift 'D' Night 6	Shift 'D' Night 7

One of the advantages of using this pattern is each shift pair, for example A and B, will get time off on weekends alternatively, because the schedule is fixed and does not drift.

DuPont 12-Hour Rotating Shift

The *DuPont 12-Hour rotating shift* provides 24/7 coverage using 4 crews and 12-hour shifts while providing a week off. Average hours is 42 per week but contains a 72-hour week which can be challenging. It is used in several manufacturing industries in the US.

DuPont 12-Hour rotating shift example:

Week	Fri	Sat	Sun	Mon	Tues	Weds	Thurs
1	Nights	Nights	Nights	Nights	Off	Off	Off
2	Days	Days	Days	Off	Nights	Nights	Nights
3	Off	Off	Off	Days	Days	Days	Days
4	Off	Off	Off	Off	Off	Off	Off

Five and Two

The *five and two* provides 24/7 coverage using 4 crews and 12-hour shifts over a fortnight. Average hours is 42 per week but contains a 60-hour week which can be challenging.

Five and two shift example:

Week	Fri	Sat	Sun	Mon	Tues	Weds	Thurs	Fri	Sat	Sun	Mon	Tues	Weds	Thurs
1	Nights	Nights	Nights	Off	Off	Nights	Nights	Off	Off	Off	Days	Days	Off	Off
2	Days	Days	Days	Off	Off	Days	Days	Off	Off	Off	Nights	Nights	Off	Off
3	Off	Off	Off	Swing	Swing	Off	Off	Swing	Swing	Swing	Off	Off	Swing	Swing
4	Off	Off	Off	Days	Days	Off	Off	Days	Days	Days	Off	Off	Days	Days

Seven-day Eight-hour Rotating Shift

The *seven-day eight-hour rotating shift* provided 24/7 coverage using 8-hour shifts with 14 crews. Consisted of a morning shift from 07:00 to 15:00, a swing shift from 15:00 to 22:30 and a night shift from 22:30 to 07:30 Each shift was worked for five days straight. The 8-hour shifts allowed vacations and absences to be covered by splitting shifts or working double shifts.

The run of day shifts was 56 hours but the 8-hour shift provided time for some socializing after work. Was once common in the pulp and paper industry in the Western United States but has been largely replaced by a 8 days, 8 swing, 5 nights, 9 off, 8-hour rotation.

Seven-day eight-hour rotating shift example:

Week	Sun	Mon	Tues	Weds	Thurs	Fri	Sat
1	Day	Day	Day	Day	Day	Off	Off
2	Swing	Off	Off	Swing	Swing	Swing	Swing
3	Night	Night	Off	Off	Night	Night	Night
4	Day	Day	Day	Day	Off	Off	Day
5	Swing	Swing	Swing	Swing	Swing	Off	Off
6	Off	Night	Night	Night	Night	Night	Off
7	Off	Off	Day	Day	Day	Day	Day
8	Swing	Swing	Swing	Swing	Swing	Off	Off
9	Night	Off	Off	Night	Night	Night	Night
10	Day	Day	Off	Off	Day	Day	Day
11	Swing	Swing	Swing	Off	Off	Swing	Swing
12	Night	Night	Night	Night	Off	Off	Night
13	Day	Day	Day	Day	Day	Off	Off
14	Off	Swing	Swing	Swing	Swing	Swing	Off
15	Off	Off	Night	Night	Night	Night	Night

Sixes

Submarine sailors in the American Navy engage in a pattern known as sixes while underway. Instead of a 24-hour day, the ship operates on an 18-hour schedule. Any given individual is scheduled to stand watch for 6 hours, perform any other duties and engage in leisure time for 6 hours, then sleep for 6 hours. If enough personnel are available, a given watchstation may benefit from a fourth man referred to as the *midnight cowboy*.

He will stand the same 6-hour watch in a given 24-hour period, usually from midnight to 06:00 (hence the *midnight* portion of the name, which is most often shortened to just *cowboy*) and the person who would normally stand that watch is free. This gives rise to a schedule of six on, twelve off, six on, thirty off, six on, twelve off.

Firefighting Schedules

In many departments, firefighters work 24-hour shifts. They are authorized to sleep in the fire station at night but are still subject to calls for service the entire shift. Departments have many options for scheduling firefighters for coverage. One option is 24 on/48 off, where a firefighter will work 24 hours and have 48 hours off, regardless of the day of the week or the holidays. Often they will be scheduled in an A–B–C pattern. Thus, a firefighter will be assigned to A, B or C shift and work whenever that letter is on the calendar.

California Roll Shift Schedule

Another option is known as a California roll, where some shifts will be close together but allow for several days off. One option is thus:

Time	Sat	Sun	Mon	Tues	Wed	Thur	Fri
Week 1 07:00 to 07:00	A	B	A	C	A	C	B
Week 2 07:00 to 07:00	C	B					

where a firefighter will work 24 hours on, 24 off, 24 on, 24 off, 24 on, 96 hours (4 days) off.

Another way to do this is:

Time	Sat	Sun	Mon	Tues	Wed	Thur	Fri
Week 1 07:00 to 07:00	A	B	A	B	C	A	C
Week 2 07:00 to 07:00	A	B	C	B	C		

where a firefighter will work one day, off one, work one, off two, work one, off four days.

Four-platoon 24-hour Shift Schedule

Another variation of the 24-hr shift schedule is a 4-platoon system, averaging 42 hours/week. Thus, the schedule is 24 on, 48 off, 24 on, 96 off, on a 4-day rotation.

Week	Mon	Tues	Wed	Thur	Fri	Sat	Sun
Week 1	A	D	B	A	C	B	D
Week 2	C	A	D	B	A	C	B
Week 3	D	C	A	D	B	A	C
Week 4	B	D	C	A	D	B	A

Another variation of this schedule is 24 on, 24 off, 24 on, 120 off, which is 1 on, 1 off, 1 on, 5 off, averaging 42 hours/ week.

Graveyard Shift

Graveyard shift, night shift or third shift (3rd shift) means a shift of work running through the early hours of the morning, especially shifts from midnight until 08:00 or from 23:00 until 07:00 There is no certainty as to the origin of this phrase; according to Michael Quinion it is little more than "an evocative term for the night shift ... when ... your skin is clammy, there's sand behind your eyeballs, and the world is creepily silent, like the graveyard."

In 2007, the World Health Organization (WHO) announced that working the graveyard shift would be listed as a "probable" cause of cancer.

HEALTH CONSEQUENCES

The February 15, 2005 issue of American Family Physician noted that shift work has been associated with cluster headaches. Health problems in the short term can also include fatigue, stress and loss of concentration, a higher rate of absence from the job and poor sexual performance, as shown in the majority of 200 variable-shift workers in a recent study in Kuwait.

Long term consequences of disturbing natural circadian rhythms have been investigated also. A study by Knutsson et al. in 1986 found that shift workers who had worked in that method for 15 years or more were 300% more likely to develop ischemic heart disease.

In 1978 Cohen et al. proposed that reduced production of the hormone melatonin might increase the risk of breast cancer, citing "environmental lighting" as a possible causal factor. Working the night shift first became associated with higher rates of cancer in 1987. This may be due to alterations in circadian rhythm: melatonin, a known tumor suppressant, is generally produced at night and late shifts may disrupt its production.

Multiple studies have documented a link between night shift work and the increased incidence of breast cancer. The WHO's International Agency for Research on Cancer listed "shiftwork that involves circadian disruption" as a probable carcinogen in 2007 (IARC Press release No. 180).

UCSF neurologist Louis Ptacek, who studies circadian rhythms, genes and sleep behaviors, has been quoted: "It's not surprising; we have evolved on a planet that is rotating every 24 hours. Our internal clock is more than just when we sleep and wake. It's related to cell division and it regulates our immune systems. When we battle our internal clock that has complications."

A good review of current knowledge of the health consequences of exposure to artificial light at night and an explanation of the causal mechanisms was published in the *Journal of Pineal Research* in 2007.

One study suggests that, for those working a night shift (such as 23:00 to 07:00), it may be advantageous to sleep in the evening (14:00 to 22:00) rather than the morning (08:00 to 16:00). The study's evening sleep subjects had 37% fewer episodes of attentional impairment than the morning sleepers.

The health consequences of shift work may depend on whether one is a day person or a night person and what shift one is assigned to.

Shift Work Management Practices

The practices and policies put in place by managers of round-the-clock or 24/7 operations can significantly influence shift worker alertness (and hence safety) and performance.

Air traffic controllers typically work an 8-hour day, 5 days per week. Research has shown that when controllers remain "in position" for more than two hours, even at low traffic levels, performance can deteriorate rapidly, so they are typically placed "in position" for 30-minute intervals (with 30 minutes between intervals).

These practices and policies can be fairly obvious: selecting an appropriate shift schedule or rota and using an employee scheduling software to maintain it, setting the length of shifts, managing overtime, increasing lighting levels, or providing shift worker lifestyle training to help shift workers better handle issues such as understanding basic circadian physiology, sleep and napping, caffeine usage, social life issues, diet and nutrition, etc.

They may also be more indirect: retirement compensation based on salary in the last few years of employment (which can encourage excessive overtime among older workers who may be less able to obtain adequate sleep), or screening and hiring of new shift workers that assesses adaptability to a shift work schedule.

Field Service Management

Field service management (FSM), also known as field force automation (FFA), is an attempt to optimize processes and information needed by companies who send technicians or staff "into the field" (or out of the office.) Optimization is difficult, since it involves intelligent scheduling and dispatching of multiple technicians to different locations daily, while minimizing cost and maintaining good customer service. FSM most commonly refers to companies who need to manage installs, service or repairs of systems or equipment.

Field service management involves a combination of some or all of the following: CRM applications, work order management, dispatch, wireless technology, and historical customer service data. Field service software combines many of these functions into one unified solution.

The software may also utilize databases containing details on customer premise equipment, access requirements, and parts inventory. Many Field Service Management solutions integrate with other software such as accounting programs like IFS Applications, QuickBooks, MYOB, SAP, Mainpac, Oracle, MFGPro etc.

Field service management creates a mobile system that connects the field worker with the backend. In turn, this type of software improves field worker productivity, enhances customer service, automates paper processes, assists with regulatory compliance, reduces human error, inventory turnover etc. In this field power scheduling is often most important because it determines how effective field service management will become.

Proper scheduling maximizes work time, minimizes travel time, matches technicians skills and certifications to the work, prioritizes work by service level agreement (SLA), consider the availability of parts, and attempts to avoid technician overtime all while maintaining an acceptable level of customer service.

"In the typical mobile field service scenario, the customer contacts the call center. A call center representative enters a work order. Once the work order is processed, the job notes, billing, and parts information from the order are automatically updated in the systems dispatch and accounting applications. This information is then sent to the relevant field technician's handheld PC, and the technician performs the work. In the case of a problem, the technician can use the handheld device to communicate with the dispatch center directly. The dispatchers thus have real-time, accurate status information about any technician or work order."

9

Human Resources Personal in Hotel Industry

Many businesses in the hospitality industry - both small and large have difficulty in understanding their human resource and employment relations obligations whichever country or countries they operate in!

Human Resources are the essential factor of success for a business – and this applies in particular to a service-providing business. Therefore, the aim of Lindner's employment policy is to promote the knowledge and skills, the capability of enthusiasm and the motivation of the staff in order to use the potential for continuous improvement and enhancement of performance and quality.

EXCELLENT MANAGEMENT IN LEARNING STRUCTURES

Each year, the staff members and the senior management agree on clear, ambitious, and inspiring *aims*. Our senior executives leave the staff members decision margins and communicate in a credible and reliable way. Their management is based on confidence and they enhance an exemplary exchange of knowledge. Curiosity, the ability to learn, the spirit of a pioneer and an open mind make that we actively contribute to design the future to the benefit of everyone.

An efficient ***assessment system*** enables the senior management of Lindner Hotels AG to help each staff member find out its fortes and to promote him/her accordingly.

With each other, not against each other: *The Lindner Dialogue*

Cooperation between the different divisions of our business in the scope of the institutionalised ***Lindner Dialogue*** which consists of several elements is no "one-way communication" but a dialogue of equal partners:

Workshops, where new tools and procedures are worked out Regular ***Operations Meetings*** and ***Strategy Meetings*** guarantee a common view on the challenges which lie ahead of us

Thanks to this contribution of different views and knowledge, we succeed in steadily developing our business. And in addition, we reach a high degree of acceptance for the ideas worked out in common.

Entry into the business facilitated—During the training period, each new staff member is assigned a colleague ***sponsor*** from his/her own department who helps and assists him/her in the beginning.

In addition, new staff members are given the possibility of participating in an ***introduction (close-up)*** organized to get to know the entire business and the individual persons who are behind it. This way, the new start in our business is facilitated to each new staff member.

STAFF DEVELOPMENT ACTIONS

In order to promote the employees adequately, special actions are required. Within Lindner Hotels AG, we offer you the possibility of individually realizing your career by participating in vocational and comprehensive ***trainings*** in regular intervals. You have in addition the possibility of taking part in an ***Inhouse - Cross Training*** offering you the opportunity to gain more flexibility through changing spheres of functions, to broaden your range of employment possibilities and achieve a higher position. Moreover, there is the possibility of using the Lindner Hotels AG inhouse ***Job Market*** for a change of post to change and develop within the business.

It's understood that at any point of time you have the possibility of planning your personal career in ***consulting career discussions*** with the central Human Resources Management or with your superior in line.

Promotion of Young Potentials and High Potentials

We take a particular interest in the promotion of young management trainees, our "rough diamonds", whom we identify at an early stage of their career by means of ***potential analysis and development dialogues*** which take place on an annual basis. We give them tailor-made individualised ***promotion and training programs*** which may be extensive in-house programs as well as specific ***management staff trainings.***

Joint Visions

In regular intervals, all the staff members of our hotels are invited to participate in joint meetings ***(Come togethers)***. In these meetings, they are informed on the objectives of the hotel company and on important activities. The prizes awarded for ***staff proposals*** we received are presented and discussed in order to attain to new solutions and goals in common. This way, joint visions for the future of our business are developped and energies are steered into a common direction.

This is understandable given the raft of legislation and regulations governing (drowning) the employment environment in which governments seem to revel in.

The hospitality industry is certainly no exception and in many cases is more complex than the average business.

We will outline important employment matters that will assist in reducing the 'stress' factors you may be experiencing directly related to the hospitality industry which Biz Momentum is actively involved in a hands on capacity.

It has been reliably estimated that 75% of businesses do not have an employee agreements and employment related policies & procedures. In the event of a dispute the law will decide for you and this almost always goes against you, the employer;

Worldwide bullying and sexual harassment claims are escalating. The average cost of a claim is $36,500 - $250,000 and recently in one country an employee was awarded $1,000,000. This comes directly off your bottom line profit;

Workplace rape and sodomy is on the increase in the hospitality industry and we have witnessed the resultant trauma, ill will and bad publicity for your hotel, restaurant or workplace where this occurred;

Workplace stalking through employees following, sending emails, voice messages and gifts is becoming more prevalent and is resulting in increased absenteeism and resignations;

Theft of your inventory such as quality wine, food and equipment is rampant!

Misuse and unlawful use of your facilities for personal gain is increasing;

It has been reliably proven that some employees use up to 2 hours per day of your email and internet facilities for personal gain and to access unlawful sites such as hate literature and pornography not to mention chat lines.

Many hotel and restaurants deliberately flout occupational health and safety rules which is resulting in increased staff turn over, fines and costly pay-outs to employees;

Many managers do not understand or have the experience in the know how of how to manage and lead employees. People skills a re paramount to your business success.

Not having an adequate job description and controlling management behaviours can be a cause of psychological injury resulting in hefty fines not to mention the process of litigation which we have seen take up to 3 years to resolve

This is far from an exhaustive list but covers a number of growing issues in which Biz Momentum has noticed in recent years affecting the hospitality industry.

The 'Basic Ingredients' for managing employment risks: There are certain steps you can take to minimise your employment risks. Biz Momentum have provided some general employment advice regarding managing employment risks however we need to advise you that each business has its own unique profile and therefore decisions must be made on that businesses individual merits.

1. Job Descriptions—A simple yet effectively written job description cannot be overlooked when hiring an employee or manager.

Employees and management need to understand what they are responsible and accountable for as well as what core skills they require to safely perform their duties.

The Restaurant who thought paperwork was a waste of time—Recently a restaurant was sued by an employee for $325,000 for psychological injury. The employee had worked in their position for two years and asserted that they had been injured because they didn't receive a job description.

The matter is proceeding to court with attorneys appointed on both sides.

The claim is completely spurious and yet the legal system is set up so that the employee will be compensated. The business did not have a job description. Employees are more inclined now to take you on and engage contingency fee lawyers to sue you (no win – no fee lawyers)

It is not only the cost of litigation but preparation, meetings, affidavits, interviews and stress on the business owner.

2. Employment Agreements—An employment agreement sets out the boundaries and expectations of the employment relationship and is a critical document for the protection of your business.

Employment agreements must contain employee benefits and obligations. Failure in having a well written employment agreement leaves you open to the courts and tribunals interpreting your obligations for you.

The hospitality industry in diverse with many different types of employees in-house. Every employee from the cleaner to maid, front of house, head chef and apprentices, wait staff, maintenance workers, office workers and all others must have a job description otherwise you face stiff penalties when things such as accidents and incidents all goes wrong.

Common clause include hours, leave, goodwill, business records, restraints for management, confidentiality, intellectual property, remuneration and benefits, requirements of the position, privacy, ethical constraints, use of business assets, warranties, responsibilities and much more.

There are many types of agreements that your business can choose from but each business must be assessed on its own circumstances and merits.

Hotel Partner that Changed their Mind—A hotel's business was severely impacted when a Partner working in a boutique hotel for 5 years left and the other partners had not bothered arranging an agreement or restrictive covenant clause as the Partner after he made it clear that after a 3 year term he would be travelling overseas for some time.

However the person changed their mind when they began a personal relationship in the local city. Subsequently the partner left the hotel and started there own business around the corner.

The original hotel and restaurant lost a great deal of their previously loyal patronage. It is not uncommon for customers to quickly find out you have lost a key person in your business and follow them elsewhere.

This was a very costly error resulting in much goodwill and profit leaving the business. This could have easily been averted by ensuring that all parties signed a well written Partnership and Employment containing restraints, ownership of goodwill to name a few clauses.

Now may be a good time to ensure you have up to date employee agreements for all levels of employees including senior management. Senior Management is often overlooked and this is to your peril. The days of trust are disappearing where your best employee today can be your worst enemy tomorrow if things go wrong.

Imagine the consequences to your business if this happened to YOU.

4. Policies and Procedures—A human resources policy and procedures manual is an essential tool protecting your business only if the manual is implemented and used appropriately.

Failure to implement effective policies and procedures and to comply with them will result in the courts and tribunals interpreting your obligations for you in what will be an expensive exercise.

In addition not having the correct policies and procedures can constrain you from taking certain action that could have been taken in the event you have clearly stated policies and procedures.

Drug and Alcohol testing is one area that many in the hospitality industry have fallen foul of by making rash decisions and firing the employee only to find themselves being subjected to litigation.

Common policies and procedures Biz Momentum recommend for the hospitality industry include appointment policy, children at the workplace, customer/employee relationships, code of conduct, computer user policy, anti discrimination prevention, drugs and alcohol, employee dress and grooming, laptop computers and equipment, leave, use of mobile phones, motor vehicles, privacy and freedom of information, sexual harassment prevention, stress prevention, termination of employment and employee discipline, workplace harassment and workplace health and safety.

These policies must be tailored for each section of your business; eg restaurant, maintenance et al.

Case - Unfair Dismissal & Sexual Harassment—In another unsatisfactory situation an employee was dismissed for consistent poor performance. Her Lawyer subsequently suggested that she sue the employer for unfair dismissal and sexual harassment.

Clearly this is extremely stressful for the business owner.

The situation could have easily been averted by a discipline and termination policy and procedure and a Sexual Harassment Prevention Policy.

Sexual harassment and workplace bullying are rapidly immerging as one of the scourges of all businesses and in our experience it is particularly prevalent in some sectors of the hospitality industry.

Biz Momentum has assisted the hospitality industry in advising in situations of workplace rape and sodomy from an employment perspective. Naturally all such incidences should be referred to the authorities for investigation.

However you are required to have a workplace rehabilitation assistance program in place should the person be willing to return to work or not and that's just a start of what you must do.

5. Induction Process—Inducting employees into your 'Business' should be structured process! Your employees are taken through your Business policies, procedures and work manuals in a formal manner.

Whether Management or line staff they must complete the process with a sign off procedure to say they have understood the requirement to comply with your policies and procedures.

The importance of this process cannot be overstated. Recently we assisted a business who was being sued for $300,000 for an employee asserting they had not been inducted and the employee lost because the business could produce and prove that induction had taken place.

Biz Momentum can takes you through an induction process that is streamlined and takes less than 1 - 4 hours for a new employee depending on the size and complexity of your business. Biz Momentum often conducts inductions on behalf of the business as we are considered experts in this area.

Case – The Thief, the Wine, the Video Line—In yet another seemingly open and shut case a well known hotel business owner caught the head chief of his restaurant stealing a bottle of quality wine via video taping that was operating in this hotel.

Angry at the theft the hotel owner sought to instantly dismiss the employee and decided to take advice at the last moment with Biz Momentum.

This was a good decision on his part. Even though the owner had video proof of the employee's theft the owner was still obliged to allow the person caught stealing the opportunity to 'show cause' or tell him why he should not have been dismissed. This is commonly referred to as natural justice: allowing the person to put their side of the matter to you.

Secondly the hotel did not induct its employees that they were subject to video surveillance which proved to be a problem for the hotel.

The hotel owner subsequently decided to issue the head chef a written warning and the head chef subsequently resigned. This was a good outcome for the hotel, a good lesson to its other employees as well as protecting the owner from potential litigation.

The moral of this case study is that you must be wise and take advice and consider all the facts (theft and surveillance were not the only issues) before you fire an employee.

6. Communication—Communication is the oil that makes a business work effectively and efficiently. Most grapevines and gossip thrive in a communications vacuum.

Be quick to correct your concerns on a day to day basis with your employees and avoid the cost of procrastination whereby time and emotion now interplays and the issue gets all blown out of all proportion.

We can show you how!

7. Reward and recognition—We all appreciate a 'thank you' and 'well done' from our customers and other people who matter to us. Employees are no different and regular positive feedback at times reinforced by a tangible reward goes a long way towards establishing a culture of trust and high morale.

We all know that costs are increasing however develop a generous spirit with your employees and ensure they are remunerated fairly and well.

The reward to you will be diminished turnover and a good reputation. Studies have shown many of your employees will remain with you because of the work environment and morale even when they are headhunted with a better offer. Money is not always the key dominant factor in retaining valuable employees.

Many managers try the carrot and the stick approach to managing employees and it has been estimated that up to 60% of managers are ill equipped to manage people and are seriously lacking common skills such as courtesy, understanding, tack and listening skills.

It's really like letting a bull run rampant through a china shop. The disaster becomes apparent and it is often too late to fix.

Biz Momentum has many years experience in advising businesses in employment issues. We regularly conduct seminars to educate business owners in their obligations and have assisted many businesses in the hospitality industry with practical solutions, training and mentoring in employment matters and have undertaken international work where requested and resources are available.

HUMAN RESOURCES

Human resources are a term used to describe the individuals who make up the workforce of an organization, although it is also applied in labor economics to, for example, business sectors or even whole nations.

Human resources is also the name of the function within an organization charged with the overall responsibility for implementing strategies and policies relating to the management of individuals (i.e. the human resources). This function title is often abbreviated to the initials "HR".

Human resources is a relatively modern management term, coined as early as the 1960s - when humanity took a shift as human rights came to a brighter light during the Vietnam Era. The origins of the function arose in organizations that introduced 'welfare management' practices and also in those that adopted the principles of 'scientific management'. From these terms emerged a largely administrative management activity, coordinating a range of worker related processes and becoming known, in time, as the 'personnel function'.

Human resources progressively became the more usual name for this function, in the first instance in the United States as well as multinational or international corporations, reflecting the adoption of a more quantitative as well as strategic approach to workforce management, demanded by corporate management to gain a competitive advantage, utilizing limited skilled and highly skilled workers.

Purpose and Role

In simple terms, an organization's human resource management strategy should maximize return on investment in the organization's human capital and minimize financial risk.

Human resource managers seek to achieve this by aligning the supply of skilled and qualified individuals and the capabilities of the current workforce, with the organization's ongoing and future business plans and requirements to maximize return on investment and secure future survival and success.

In ensuring such objectives are achieved, the human resource function is to implement an organization's human resource requirements effectively, taking into account federal, state and local labor laws and regulations; ethical business practices; and net cost, in a manner that maximizes, as far as possible, employee motivation, commitment and productivity.

Key Functions

Human Resources may set strategies and develop policies, standards, systems, and processes that implement these strategies in a whole range of areas. The following are typical of a wide range of organizations:

- Maintaining awareness of and compliance with local, state and federal labor laws (Department of Labor federal labor law information)
- Recruitment, selection, and on boarding (resourcing)
- Employee recordkeeping and confidentiality
- Organizational design and development
- Business transformation and change management
- Performance, conduct and behavior management
- Industrial and employee relations
- Human resources (workforce) analysis and workforce personnel data management
- Compensation and employee benefit management
- Training and development (learning management)
- Employee motivation and morale-building (employee retention and loyalty)

Implementation of such policies, processes or standards may be directly managed by the HR function itself, or the function may indirectly supervise the implementation of such activities by managers, other business functions or via third-party external partner organizations. Applicable legal issues, such as the potential for disparate treatment and disparate impact, are also extremely important to HR managers.

In organizations, it is important to determine both current and future organizational requirements for both core employees and the contingent workforce in terms of their skills/technical abilities, competencies, flexibility etc. The analysis requires consideration of the internal and external factors that can have an effect on the resourcing, development, motivation and retention of employees and other workers.

External factors are those largely outside the control of the organization. These include issues such as economic climate and current and future labor market trends (e.g., skills, education level, government investment into industries etc.). On the other hand, internal influences are broadly controlled by the organization to predict, determine, and monitor—for example—the organizational culture, underpinned by management style, environmental climate, and the approach to ethical and corporate social responsibilities.

Major Trends

To know the business environment an organization operates in, three major trends must be considered:

1. Demographics: the characteristics of a population/ workforce, for example, age, gender or social class. This type of trend may have an effect in relation to pension offerings, insurance packages etc.
2. Diversity: the variation within the population/ workplace. Changes in society now mean that a larger proportion of organizations are made up of "baby-boomers" or older employees in comparison to thirty years ago. Advocates of "workplace diversity" simply advocate an employee base that is a mirror reflection of the make-up of society insofar as race, gender, sexual orientation etc.
3. Skills and qualifications: as industries move from manual to more managerial professions so does the need for more highly skilled graduates. If the market is "tight" (i.e. not enough staff for the jobs), employers must compete for employees by offering financial rewards, community investment, etc.

Individual Responses

In regard to how individuals respond to the changes in a labor market, the following must be understood:

- Geographical spread: how far is the job from the individual? The distance to travel to work should be in line with the pay offered, and the transportation and infrastructure of the area also influence who applies for a post.

- Occupational structure: the norms and values of the different careers within an organization. Mahoney 1989 developed 3 different types of occupational structure, namely, craft (loyalty to the profession), organization career (promotion through the firm) and unstructured (lower/unskilled workers who work when needed).
- Generational difference: different age categories of employees have certain characteristics, for example, their behavior and their expectations of the organization.

Framework

Human Resources Development is a framework for the expansion of human capital within an organization or (in new approaches) a municipality, region, or nation. Human Resources Development is a combination of training and education, in a broad context of adequate health and employment policies, that ensures the continual improvement and growth of both the individual, the organization, and the national human resourcefulness.

Adam Smith states, "The capacities of individuals depended on their access to education".Human Resources Development is the medium that drives the process between training and learning in a broadly fostering environment. Human Resources Development is not a defined object, but a series of organised processes, "with a specific learning objective" (Nadler,1984)Within a national context, it becomes a strategic approach to inter sectoral linkages between health, education and employment.

Structure

Human Resources Development is the structure that allows for individual development, potentially satisfying the organization's, or the nation's goals. Development of the individual benefits the individual, the organization—and the nation and its citizens. In the corporate vision, the Human Resources Development framework views employees as an asset to the enterprise, whose value is enhanced by development, "Its primary focus is on growth and employee development...it emphasizes developing individual potential and skills."

Human Resources Development in this treatment can be in-room group training, tertiary or vocational courses or mentoring and coaching by senior employees with the aim for a desired outcome that develops the individual's performance. At the level of a national strategy, it can be a broad inter-sectoral approach to fostering creative contributions to national productivity.

Training and Development

At the organizational level, a successful Human Resources Development program prepares the individual to undertake a higher level of work, "organized learning over a given period of time, to provide the possibility of performance change" (Nadler 1984). In these settings, Human Resources Development is the framework that focuses on the organization's competencies at the first stage, training, and then developing the employee, through education, to satisfy the organization's long-term needs and the individual's career goals and employee value to their present and future employers. Human Resources Development can be defined simply as developing the most important section of any business, its human resource, by attaining or upgrading employee skills and attitudes at all levels to maximize enterprise effectiveness.The people within an organization are its human resource.

Human Resources Development from a business perspective is not entirely focused on the individual's growth and development; "development occurs to enhance the organization's value, not solely for individual improvement. Individual education and development is a tool and a means to an end, not the end goal itself" (Elwood F. Holton II, James W. Trott Jr).The broader concept of national and more strategic attention to the development of human resources is beginning to emerge as newly independent countries face strong competition for their skilled professionals and the accompanying brain-drain they experience.

Recruitment and Selection

Applicant recruitment and employee selection form a major part of an organization's overall resourcing strategies, which identify and secure people needed for the organization to survive and succeed in the short- to medium-term. Recruitment activities need to be responsive to the increasingly competitive market to secure suitably qualified and capable recruits at all levels.

To be effective, these initiatives need to include how and when to source the best recruits, internally or externally. Common to the success of either are: well-defined organizational structures with sound job design, robust task and person specification and versatile selection processes, reward, employment relations and human resource policies, underpinned by a commitment for strong employer branding and employee engagement and onboarding strategies.

Internal recruitment can provide the most cost-effective source for recruits if the potential of the existing pool of employees has been enhanced through training, development and other performance-enhancing activities such as performance appraisal, succession planning and development centres to review performance and assess employee development needs and promotional potential.

Increasingly, securing the best quality candidates for almost all organizations relies, at least occasionally if not substantially, on external recruitment methods. Rapidly changing business models demand skill and experience that cannot be sourced or rapidly enough developed from the existing employee base. It would be unusual for an organization to undertake all aspects of the recruitment process without support from third-party dedicated recruitment firms.

This may involve a range of support services, such as: provision of CVs or resumes, identifying recruitment media, advertisement design and media placement for job vacancies, candidate response handling, shortlisting, conducting aptitude testing, preliminary interviews or reference and qualification verification.

Typically, small organizations may not have in-house resources or, in common with larger organizations, may not possess the particular skill-set required to undertake a specific recruitment assignment. Where requirements arise, these are referred on an ad hoc basis to government job centres or commercially-run employment agencies.

Except in sectors where high-volume recruitment is the norm, an organization faced with sudden, unexpected requirements for an unusually large number of new recruits often delegates the task to a specialist external recruiter. Sourcing executive-level and senior management as well as the acquisition of scarce or 'high-potential' recruits has been a long-established market serviced by a wide range of 'search and selection' or 'headhunting' consultancies, which typically form long-standing relationships with their client organizations.

Finally, certain organizations with sophisticated HR practices have identified a strategic advantage in outsourcing complete responsibility for all workforce procurement to one or more third-party recruitment agencies or consultancies. In the most sophisticated of these arrangements the external recruitment services provider may not only physically locate, or 'embed', their resourcing team(s) in the client organization's orfices, but work in tandem with the senior human resource management team in developing the longer-term HR resourcing strategy and plan.

OTHER CONSIDERATIONS

Despite its more everyday use, terms such as "human resources" and, similarly, "human capital" continue to be perceived negatively and may be considered insulting. They create the impression that people are merely commodities, like office machines or vehicles, despite assurances to the contrary.

Modern analysis emphasizes that human beings are not "commodities" or "resources", but are creative and social beings in a productive enterprise. The 2000 revision of ISO 9001, in contrast, requires identifying the processes, their sequence and interaction, and to define and communicate responsibilities and authorities. In general, heavily unionised nations such as France and Germany have adopted and encouraged such approaches. Also, in 2001, the International Labour Organization decided to revisit and revise its 1975 Recommendation 150 on Human Resources Development.

One view of these trends is that a strong social consensus on political economy and a good social welfare system facilitates labor mobility and tends to make the entire economy more productive, as labor can develop skills and experience in various ways, and move from one enterprise to another with little controversy or difficulty in adapting. Another view is that governments should become more aware of their national role in facilitating human resources development across all sectors. which includes following

Trans-national Labor Mobility

An important controversy regarding labor mobility illustrates the broader philosophical issue with usage of the phrase "human resources". Governments of developing nations often regard developed nations that encourage immigration or "guest workers" as appropriating human capital that is more rightfully part of the developing nation and required to further its economic growth.

Over time, the United Nations have come to more generally support the developing nations' point of view, and have requested significant offsetting "foreign aid" contributions so that a developing nation losing human capital does not lose the capacity to continue to train new people in trades, professions, and the arts.

Ethical Management

In the very narrow context of corporate "human resources" management, there is a contrasting pull to reflect and require workplace diversity that echoes the diversity of a global customer base. Such programs require foreign language and culture skills, ingenuity, humor, and careful listening. These indicate a general shift through the human capital point of view to an acknowledgment that human beings contribute more to a productive enterprise than just "work": they bring their character, ethics, creativity, social connections and, in some cases, pets and children, and alter the character of a workplace. The term corporate culture is used to characterize such processes at the organizational level.

The definition of an industry sector is a critical component of performing research and discussion about that sector. Thus, an industry sector is usually defined in such a way that the main parts of the sector are encapsulated in the definition, and further work for the sector is rooted in those areas. However, when discussing the hospitality sector, it is difficult to find easily defined borders for just such a definition.

The hospitality industry covers a wide ranging number of services and activities. It includes travel related services such as lodging, restaurants, food services and convention centers. Also included are entertainment services including golf courses, sports arenas, amusement parks, movie theaters, play houses, concert venues, tour services, and national and state parks, to name but a few. The hospitality industry, in its many formats, is a sector in which pollution prevention (P2) practices can have both an immediate and long-term impact. For the purposes of this document, we have chosen to focus on just a few of the areas within the hospitality sector, including lodging and tourism, golf courses, energy and water efficiency, and restaurants.

When addressing P2 in the hospitality industry, there are two basic routes that can be followed:

Implementing P2 as an add-on to already established facilities, practices, and procedures, or

Incorporating it into the building practices and culture during the design stage

Much of the early P2 work in the sector has been accomplished by implementing P2 within existing structures and procedures, and there is an extensive network of resources available to assist facilities on getting started. One such program is the Environmental Protection Agency's (EPA) Water Alliances for Voluntary Efficiency (WAVE), a program dedicated to efficient water use. WAVE goals include:

(a) Reducing water and energy consumption through the installment of water-efficient equipment

(b Linking water-use efficiency to reduced costs

(c) Informing hotel guests and employees about the benefits of water efficiency

10

Problem-Solving Practices

We've all heard that old saw that "practice makes perfect." This is hardly true. A practice is unlike a rule, guideline, principle or commandment. A practice is what a leader embraces as part of his or her development of their entrepreneurial competencies. The reality is that perfection is rarely the outcome; however, continuous improvement frequently is. A practice is an approach, a movement toward, rather than a destination in and of itself. We recently conducted research that identified the six practices to becoming a more effective hotel entrepreneur.

As the service sector continues to expand in today's economy, the hospitality industry also experiences rapid growth accompanied by a heightened demand for superior customer service and a stronger need for process optimization. This benchmarking report offers insights and guiding practices for hotel managers who seek to improve or redesign internal operations with the goal of gaining and retaining customers; building a stable, service-oriented workforce; and optimizing overall hotel profitability.

The hospitality industry is of central importance to the overall Caribbean economy and the competition for tourism dollars among the islands is growing intensively. This report outlines the productivity measures and lessons learned for managing hotel operations successfully while taking into account unique attributes of the Caribbean economy and culture.

Chapters in the report highlight best practices and metrics for operational performance; customer service excellence; personnel development; and marketing excellence.

This benchmarking study employed a two-pronged data gathering approach. The field research team designed and conducted a performance benchmark survey that gathered statistical insights from nine of the participating hotels, representing a cross-section of the industry. The research team then conducted in-depth interviews with more than 15 key functional leaders at 10 participating hotels to harvest qualitative insights, process excellence observations and managerial lessons learned.

The report evaluates multiple fronts of hotel operations that have greatest impact on customer service excellence. Some areas are directly related, such as training staff for attentiveness and courteousness in guest interactions, and effectively managing complaints. Other areas are indirectly related, but no less important. Incentives and recognition programs, for example, help sustain staff energy and morale so that customer service levels are maintained over the long-term.

Well-planned, yield-management systems help managers maximize profit in high and low seasons, anticipate swings in business and plan for staff and resources accordingly, so that the customer experience remains consistent. Fully realized marketing plans help managers define the customer segments most important to their financial and strategic goals and enable them to plan accordingly.

While any one of these areas could be benchmarked fully in its own right, a complete overview study seemed the most applicable way to suggest improvements that would improve productivity overall.

TEN MAJOR HOTEL PROBLEMS

Goal: To recognize the types of problems that are normal at different price levels.

There are benefits to a room, and there are problems, this pages is to help you understand the problems.

I have lived approximately 800 Hotel rooms in my life, and have traveled perpetually for 13 years and visited 89 countries, I am a professional traveler.

- Andy Graham of HoboTraveler.com

Types of Rooms

Bed & Breakfast

Backpacker Hostel

Boutique Hotel

Guest House

Hotel

Lodge

Private Home

Resort

Self-Catering

Types of Room that infers Better Quality and Higher Price

Luxury - Expensive

Business

Motels

Economy

Hostels

Private Home - Cheapest

Problems by Hotel Budget

0-10 US Dollars per Day - Backpacker 1-6 Month Trips

10-25 US Dollars per Day - Experienced Travelers - Less than 30 Days

25-100 -US Dollars per Day - Volunteers - Missionaries - Flashpackers - NGO - Less than 30 Days

100-150 US Dollars per Day - Tourist - Package Tours - NGO - 5-21 Days

150-200 US Dollars per Day - Business Travelers - Government Workers - United Nations - 0-14 Days

200-300 US Dollars per Day - Resort - Maybe not good at buying value Tourist - 0 - 14 Days

300-500 US Dollars per Day - Resort - Short Trips

Over 500 US Dollars per Day - Luxury 14 Days

0-10 US Dollars per Day - Backpacker 1-6 Month Trips (and) - Same

10-25 US Dollars per Day - Experienced Travelers - Less than 30 Days

Anything from list of Hotel problems will happen at this level, and should be allowed, at this level you need to know your personal major problems and avoid them. For example, car noise is difficult for me, so my high priority is to avoid this.

1. Carpet Smells of Cat
2. Permanent sag or dent in mattress
3. Car of Truck Traffic
4. Receptionist Play Music or do annoying behavior.
5. Unhelpful staff
6. Animals, Dog, Cats and Chickens
7. Construction working being done at hotel or close.
8. Churches, Mosques Make Noise
9. No Electricity or Brown Outs
10. Floor Fan is Missing Plug
11. Floor Fan is Broken
12. Noise coming from plumbing or sanitary pipes as water comes down from upper floors.
13. Fan in Center of Ceiling too Slow
14. Fan in Center of Ceiling does not Work

15. Fan in Center of Ceiling only has one speed
16. Fan in Center of Ceiling Squeaks
17. Light Bulbs Burned Out
18. Transom Above Door is Screen and Noise is Loud
19. Rock and Roll Bands
20. Staff steals when cleaning the room
21. Overcharged
22. Ants
23. Mosquitoes
24. No Mosquito Net
25. Spiders
26. Mice or Rats
27. Cockroaches
28. No labels on hot or cold, no on or off.
29. Furniture is in wrong location.
30. Never offer to clean the room or change the sheets.

25-100 -US Dollars per Day

- Volunteers - Missionaries - Flashpackers - NGO - Less than 30 Days

The pivotal benefit to find at this level is screens on windows and hot water, if these two benefits are missing, you should pay less than 25 Dollars per night.

1. Screens on Windows to Stop Mosquitoes
2. Tour Buses with Large Groups Making Noise
3. Unhelpful staff
4. No fresh air because of air conditioning and you have sinus or breathing problems.
5. No way to wash clothes and none provided
6. Courtyard windows facing so you can hear TV, People in other rooms

7. Maintenance Never Done
8. Air Conditioners Blows directly at Bed or Eyes of person sleeping
9. Air Conditioner is Noisy
10. Plumbing Traps missing on Sink or Shower Drains
11. Tourist Traps that are too close
12. Group Rents the complete Hotel and makes noise or you have to move.
13. Ceiling is too High and Air Conditioner does not Cool Room
14. Remote Control on Televisions does not work
15. No security box big enough for computer or camera.
16. No booking on arrival or Overbooked
17. WIFI or Internet Access only in Common Areas
18. There is No Sign to Hang on Door Requesting Room to be Cleaned

100-150 US Dollars per Day - Tourist - Package Tours - NGO - 5-21 Days

The pivotal benefit at this level is you will have extreme quiet, peace, and all the travelers nest should be serviced.

1. No security box big enough for computer or camera.
2. Staff steals when cleaning the room
3. Tour Sales People Hanging out in front of Hotel
4. Housecleaning ignores sign and clean room when sign posted to not clean
5. Tourist Traps that are too close
6. Staff is Indifferent and Non-Caring
7. Too far from infrastructure of city
8. No fresh air because of air conditioning and you have sinus or breathing problems.
9. No way to wash clothes and none provided

10. Bums - Beggars Waiting or Hanging out in front of Hotel
11. WIFI or Internet Access only in Common Areas

150-200 US Dollars per Day

- Business Travelers - Government Workers - United Nations - 0-14 Days;

The pivotal benefit to find is a Business Center and a wonderful view of something, this is the level where luxuries are prevalent, swimming pools and massage.

1. No security box big enough for computer or camera.
2. Taxis are Overpriced just outside door to Hotel and no way to get proper priced Tax
3. Staff is Indifferent and Non-Caring
4. No fresh air because of air conditioning and you have sinus or breathing problems.
5. No Scales to Weigh Luggage
6. WIFI or Internet Access only in Common Areas
7. Overcharged

200-300 US Dollars per Day

- Resort - Maybe not good at buying value Tourist - 0 - 14 Days

This is the level where there is no reason to leave the Hotel or Resort, all your needs should be met including laundry, food and communication, if you have to leave you are paying too much, this includes tours, plane tickets and money exchange.

1. Taxis are Overpriced just outside door to Hotel and no way to get proper priced Taxi
2. Remote Control on Televisions does not work
3. Mini bar scam
4. Hotel Occupied by One Culture or Country and Dominate

5. Staff Does Not Arrange Taxis
6. Sub Standard restaurant
7. Inaccurate star rating
8. No Scales to Weigh Luggage
9. No Health Center or Not Open at Sufficient Hours
10. No security box big enough for computer or camera.
11. No Prices on Services
12. Overcharged
13. No Business Center

300-500 US Dollars per Day - Resort - Short Trips

1. Remote Control on Televisions does not work
2. Taxis are Overpriced just outside door to Hotel and no way to get proper priced Taxi
3. You assumed more money was better.
4. Hotel Occupied by One Culture or Country and Dominate
5. Overcharged
6. Mini bar scam
7. Sub Standard restaurant
8. Women are told they cannot be Topless
9. Inaccurate star rating
10. People are too Old to be Fun
11. Business Center People are not Educated Sufficiently
12. No Health Center or Not Open at Sufficient Hours
13. There is no way to meet real locals, the staff constantly channels you away from common people and lie.

Over 500 US Dollars per Day - Luxury 14 Days

- This is the level where debauchery is allowed, can what you do is your moral responsibility. This is where Kings and Queens can relax and have an affair and all will be kept private. "What happens in this Hotel, stays in this Hotel."

The moral standards of the country are not enforced inside the Hotel.

1. Too far from infrastructure of city
2. People are too Old to be Fun
3. Business Center People are not Educated Sufficiently
4. There is no way to meet real locals, the staff constantly channels you away from common people and lie.
5. Getting Special Assistants and Language assistants are sub-standard.
6. The customer is always right is not understood by the local culture.
7. No Place to Park the Sailboat or Yacht
8. Concierge Refuses to Arrange for Men or Women Lovers to come to Room

Hostels Have Special Problem

1. Lockers are Not Secure, and Staff Has Access
2. Forced to Leave During Day
3. Drunks Coming in and Out of Dorm
4. Staff is Indifferent and Non-Caring
5. Hotel Occupied by One Culture or Country and Dominate
6. People in the Dorm Having Sex
7. Staff Robs all the Lockers
8. Staff Robs Backpack While forcing you to Leave for Day
9. People in Dormitory Rob ÿþYou
10. Hours Open is not 24 Hours

List of Worst to Least Problem - This includes all type of Travel Rooms

1. Carpet Smells of Catÿþ
2. Car of Truck Traffic
3. Receptionist Play Music or do annoying behavior.

4. Unhelpful staff
5. Animals, Dog, Cats and Chickens
6. Construction working being done at hotel or close.
7. Churches, Mosques Make Noise
8. No Electricity or Brown Outs
9. Floor Fan is Missing Plug
10. Floor Fan is Broken
11. Fan in Center of Ceiling too Slow
12. Fan in Center of Ceiling does not Work
13. Fan in Center of Ceiling only has one speed
14. Fan in Center of Ceiling Squeaks
15. Light Bulbs Burned Out
16. Transom Above Door is Screen and Noise is Loud
17. Rock and Roll Bands
18. Staff steals when cleaning the room
19. Overcharged
20. Ants
21. Mosquitoes
22. No Mosquito Net
23. Spiders
24. Mice or Rats
25. Cockroaches
26. Screens on Windows to Stop Mosquitoes
27. Party by Residents in Hotel
28. Bar in the Hotel Noisy
29. Plumbing Traps missing on Sink or Shower Drains
30. Too far from infrastructure of city
31. Corrugate Tin roofs
32. Running Vehicles Parked outside of room
33. There is No Sign to Hang on Door Requesting Room to be Cleaned

34. No security box big enough for computer or camera.
35. Courtyard windows facing so you can hear TV, People in other rooms
36. Tour Buses with Large Groups Making Noise
37. People Arriving or Leaving Hotel
38. People coming home after night out
39. Common Area to close to rooms.
40. Air Conditioners Blows directly at Bed or Eyes of person sleeping
41. Air Conditioner is Noisy
42. Electrical Generator Noise
43. Hotel Occupied by One Culture or Country and Dominate
44. Maintenance Never Done
45. Remote Control on Televisions does not work
46. No fresh air because of air conditioning and you have sinus or breathing problems.
47. Group Rents the complete Hotel and makes noise or you have to move.
48. Ceiling is too High and Air Conditioner does not Cool Room
49. WIFI or Internet Access only in Common Areas
50. Toilet Leaking Noise
51. No Electrical Generator
52. No booking on arrival or Overbooked
53. No Prices on Services
54. Overpriced Phone chargesÿþ
55. Mini bar scam
56. No Business Center
57. Sex in Next Room

58. No Health Center or Not Open at Sufficient Hours
59. No Long Term Storage
60. No way to wash clothes and none provided
61. No way to adjust air conditioning
62. Taxis are Overpriced just outside door to Hotel and no way to get proper priced Taxi
63. Rooms are not breathing, they are so seal, no fresh air enters, and the new wall air conditioners do not allow.
64. No Scales to Weigh Luggage
65. No Closets
66. No Hangers in Closet
67. No Shelves
68. Dirty Hotel
69. Bums - Beggars Waiting or Hanging out in front of Hotel
70. Staff Does Not Arrange Taxis
71. Women are told they cannot be Topless
72. Tour Sales People Hanging out in front of Hotel
73. Housecleaning ignores sign and clean room when sign posted to not clean
74. Common Area Television is Occupied by Soccer of Football Viewers
75. Failure to Speak English the Language of Business
76. You assumed more money was better.
77. Bed Bugs
78. No Location in the Hotel to Read outside the Room
79. Poor Room Service
80. No Common Computer in the Lobby to Check Plane Tickets
81. Sub Standard restaurant
82. There is no way to meet real locals, the staff constantly channels you away from common people and lie.

83. Cancellation costs
84. Inaccurate Star Rating - (I see this as ludicrous, there is no true standard of Stars for Rooms on the planet, Stars are just an agreed upon Marketing Scheme.)
85. Business Center People are not Educated Sufficiently
86. People in Hotel are too young to be Fun
87. People are too Old to be Fun
88. No Place to Park the Sailboat or Yacht
89. Concierge Refuses to Arrange for Men or Women Lovers to come to Room.

Addendum of Problems

Note: Internet Access is best at the very bottom and very top, in between is a problem. Generally, a Mom and Pop hotel will provide Internet for their children, and keep it working good.

Note: Dirty Hotel is subjective, hard to evaluate, a person has to live 150 days a year in a Hotel before I could say this is an opinion worth listening too in the price range of the person.

Electrical

Electrical sockets turn off with light switch

Air Conditioner

Controlled by Owner of Hotel

Room

No Clock in Room

Borg This

No list of channels, HBO BBC CNN

There is no sunlight, a person does not know when it is day or night.

- Add Love Hotel
- Horns in Street
- Puta Hotel

The questionnaire asked hospitality operators, executives and owners to rate the level of importance of each item to successful entrepreneurship in the service and hospitality industries. The questionnaire included an open-ended section where respondents were asked to share their thoughts on the most important characteristics required of an entrepreneur, as well as recommendations for hospitality students interested in becoming entrepreneurs.

Our research surfaced six practices for thinking like a hotel owner:

INTRAPERSONAL COMMUNICATION

The intrapersonal communication practice is about communication with one's self. It includes honesty, listening skills, patience and technical skills. Honesty with one's self starts with self-awareness and self-understanding. It leads to knowing self, including your values, vision and mission; your strengths; areas that you can and need to improve; and your goals.

As important as it is to listen to others, it's equally essential to listen to self. By listening to your own inner voice, your own needs, wants, expectations, requirements, dreams and vision become clearer.

Entrepreneurs must be patient with themselves, first, and then with others. No one is perfect and we all make mistakes. Thus, patience is required to learn from mistakes. You also need patience to conceive, launch and build a business.

Hotel owners have technical skills that grow from practicing them in practical experiences. These skills include first-hand knowledge of the operations of the business, in part so others can be trained to deliver the requirements expected by both internal customers (associates) and external customers (guests).

The interpersonal communication practice includes conversations with others. The most important communication skill is listening. Listening requires empathy, demonstrated when listening to others' points of view from their perspectives.

Communicating effectively begins with a compelling vision of what you want to achieve. What do you want to create? How will you know it? And what will be happening? The vision must be effectively communicated to others so they can help achieve the vision. Communicating effectively is necessarily focused on listening to others words, as well as observing their actions. Others do the same to you. Facta non verba—your actions speak more loudly than your words.

AGILITY

The agility practice includes adaptability, autonomy, comfortable making decisions, independent and resourcefulness.

Adaptability is flexibility to change directions if something new surfaces. Adaptability is adjusting to conditions as they develop. Adaptability requires agility in the face of conditions that are under your control and external forces that aren't under the control of the owner. Adaptability is the cornerstone to surviving in today's economic challenges.

Hotel owners make decisions in keeping with the commitments they've made to grow the business. They visualize their dreams and work tenaciously to make their visions become reality. The passion of these entrepreneurs results in focused risk taking. These owners work hard and are determined to do what it takes, even if it means changing course, to achieve their future. It takes initiative to begin the process and perseverance to work more than they worked for someone else, including long hours, evenings and weekends.

CREATIVE SAVVINESS

The creative savviness practice covers creativity, intuition, inventiveness and being politically savvy. All these qualities are embodied in an entrepreneur who sets out to develop something new and innovative.

Creativity is one of the key strategies for staying ahead of your competition. Creativity is imbedded in anticipatory service, based on customer relationships transformed into customer (both internal and external) loyalty.

Savvy owners have a "sixth sense" when it comes to anticipating customers' needs and desires before the customers express them. These owners are inventive and look for unfilled needs and desires and hidden opportunities others don't see. They capitalize on the opportunities and advance their organizations. Politically savvy entrepreneurs see the connections between operating in an increasingly regulated and complex hotel industry environment, and an understanding of the hotel industry to position their business competitively.

PROBLEM-SOLVING PRAGMATISM

A hotel owner who practices being a problem-solving pragmatist is one who has knowledge of financial numbers and possesses objectivity.

Knowledge of financial numbers begins with building a realistic business and financial plan for the business, and then following it. These owners have a detailed understanding of balance sheets, budgets, cash flow, profit and loss statements and return on investment (ROI).

Entrepreneurs act objectively and make fact-based decisions. They constantly scan the environment, including market demographics, to determine which external customers have unmet needs and wants for products, services and experiences. Then they provide for these unmet customer requirements.

Pragmatic owners are realistic and practical. This practice is driven by the ability to balance the quality of personal life and work life. Entrepreneurs lead the business and do what it takes to make it successful. They also pay close attention to personal and family requirements. There must be a balance between the two areas so each can support the other and both can support the hotel owner.

Entrepreneurs are problem-solvers, a skill set that helps them be great operators. Problem-solving becomes a strategy to continuously improve all areas of the business. Problem-solving owners learn from their mistakes, from reading, by benchmarking successful businesses, being curious, asking questions and holding themselves and others accountable for achieving the desired outcomes.

LEGACY LEADER

The legacy leader practice embodies a desire to leave your mark and be significant. Entrepreneurs are focused on their vision for the future and, often, when describing a concept or product/service do so as if it already exists, even though it is still in the planning and development stages. They visualize their legacy and their wealth increasing both when they feel satisfied because services and products are delivered to create positively memorable experiences, as well as when there is financial gain for the hotel owner.

THE IMPLICATIONS

Our study presents practices for developing hospitality business entrepreneurial thoughts and behaviors, in general, and what we discovered applies to the hotel industry, in particular. The six practices identified include a wide range of characteristics, traits, attributes and skills.

Some characteristics are inherent, while others require entrepreneurial learning, training and repetition. This is where practice comes into play. Our results help to surface what capabilities and competencies individuals must continue to develop in order to achieve their goals of individual ownership or partnerships within larger hotel organizations.

Root cause Analysis

Root cause analysis (**RCA**) is a class of problem solving methods aimed at identifying the root causes of problems or events. The practice of RCA is predicated on the belief that problems are best solved by attempting to address, correct or eliminate root causes, as opposed to merely addressing the immediately obvious symptoms. By directing corrective measures at root causes, it is more probable that problem recurrence will be prevented.

However, it is recognized that complete prevention of recurrence by one corrective action is not always possible. Conversely, there may be several effective measures (methods) that address the root cause of a problem. Thus, RCA is often considered to be an iterative process, and is frequently viewed as a tool of continuous improvement.

RCA, is typically used as a reactive method of identifying event(s) causes, revealing problems and solving them. Analysis is done *after* an event has occurred. Insights in RCA may make it useful as a pro-active method. In that event, RCA can be used to *forecast* or predict probable events even *before* they occur. While one follows the other, RCA is a completely separate process to Incident Management.

Root cause analysis is not a single, sharply defined methodology; there are many different tools, processes, and philosophies for performing RCA analysis. However, several very-broadly defined approaches or "schools" can be identified by their basic approach or field of origin: safety-based, production-based, process-based, failure-based, and systems-based.

- Safety-based RCA descends from the fields of accident analysis and occupational safety and health.
- Production-based RCA has its origins in the field of quality control for industrial manufacturing.
- Process-based RCA is basically a follow-on to production-based RCA, but with a scope that has been expanded to include business processes.
- Failure-based RCA is rooted in the practice of failure analysis as employed in engineering and maintenance.
- Systems-based RCA has emerged as an amalgamation of the preceding schools, along with ideas taken from

fields such as change management, risk management, and systems analysis.

Despite the different approaches among the various schools of root cause analysis, there are some common principles. It is also possible to define several general processes for performing RCA.

General Principles of Root Cause Analysis

1. The primary aim of RCA is to identify the root cause(s) of a problem in order to create effective corrective actions that will prevent that problem from ever re-occurring, otherwise addressing the problem with virtual certainty of success. ("Success" is defined as the near-certain prevention of recurrence.)
2. To be effective, RCA must be performed systematically, usually as part of an investigation, with conclusions and root causes identified backed up by documented evidence. Usually a team effort is required.
3. There may be more than one root cause for an event or a problem, the difficult part is demonstrating the persistence and sustaining the effort required to develop them.
4. The purpose of identifying all solutions to a problem is to prevent recurrence at lowest cost in the simplest way. If there are alternatives that are equally effective, then the simplest or lowest cost approach is preferred.
5. Root causes identified depend on the way in which the problem or event is defined. Effective problem statements and event descriptions (as failures, for example) are helpful, or even required.
6. To be effective the analysis should establish a sequence of events or timeline to understand the relationships between contributory (causal) factors, root cause(s) and the defined problem or event to prevent in the future.
7. Root cause analysis can help to transform an reactive culture (that reacts to problems) into a forward-looking

culture that solves problems before they occur or escalate. More importantly, it reduces the frequency of problems occurring over time within the environment where the RCA process is used.

8. RCA is a threat to many cultures and environments. Threats to cultures often meet with resistance. There may be other forms of management support required to achieve RCA effectiveness and success. For example, and "non-punitory" policy towards problem identifiers may be required.

Notice that RCA (in steps 3, 4 and 5) forms the most critical part of successful corrective action, because it directs the corrective action at the true root cause of the problem. The root cause is secondary to the goal of prevention, but without knowing the root cause, we cannot determine what an effective corrective action for the defined problem will be.

1. Define the problem or describe the event factually
2. Gather data and evidence, classifying that along a timeline of events to the final failure or crisis.
3. Ask "why" and identify the causes associated with each step in the sequence towards the defined problem or event.
4. Classify causes into causal factors that relate to an event in the sequence, and root causes, that if applied can be agreed to have interrupted that step of the sequence chain.
5. If there are multiple root causes, which is often the case, reveal those clearly for later optimum selection.
6. Identify corrective action(s) that will prevent absolutely with certainty prevent recurrence of the problem or event. These can be used to select the best correction action, later
7. Identify solutions that effective, prevent recurrence with reasonable certainty with consensus agreement of the group, are within your control, meet your goals

and objectives and do not cause introduce other new, unforeseen problems.

8. Implement the recommended root cause correction(s).
9. Ensure effectiveness by observing the implemented recommendation solutions.
10. Other methodologies for problem solving and problem avoidance may be useful.

Root Cause Analysis Techniques

- Barrier analysis - a technique often used in process industries. It is based on tracing energy flows, with a focus on barriers to those flows, to identify how and why the barriers did not prevent the energy flows from causing harm.
- Bayesian inference
- Causal factor tree analysis - a technique based on displaying causal factors in a tree-structure such that cause-effect dependencies are clearly identified.
- Change analysis - an investigation technique often used for problems or accidents. It is based on comparing a situation that does not exhibit the problem to one that does, in order to identify the changes or differences that might explain why the problem occurred.
- Current Reality Tree - A method developed by Eliahu M. Goldratt in his theory of constraints that guides an investigator to identify and relate all root causes using a cause-effect tree whose elements are bound by rules of logic (Categories of Legitimate Reservation). The CRT begins with a brief list of the undesirables things we see around us, and then guides us towards one or more root causes. This method is particularly powerful when the system is complex, there is no obvious link between the observed undesirable things, and a deep understanding of the root cause(s) is desired.
- Failure mode and effects analysis

- Fault tree analysis
- 5 Whys ask why why why why over until exhausted
- Ishikawa diagram, also known as the fishbone diagram or cause-and-effect diagram. The Ishikawa diagram is for project managers for conducting RCA.
- Pareto analysis "80/20 rule"
- RPR Problem Diagnosis - An ITIL-aligned method for diagnosing IT problems.
- Kepner-Tregoe Approach

Common cause analysis (CCA) common modes analysis (CMA) are evolving engineering techniques for complex technical systems to determine if common root causes in hardware, software or highly integrated systems interaction may contribute to human error or improper operation of a system.

Systems are analyzed for root causes and causal factors to determine probability of failure modes, fault modes, or common mode software faults due to escaped requirements. Also ensuring complete testing and verification are methods used for ensuring complex systems are designed with no common causes that cause severe hazards.

Common cause analysis are sometimes required as part of the safety engineering tasks for theme parks, commercial/ military aircraft, spacecraft, complex control systems, large electrical utility grids, nuclear power plants, automated industrial controls, medical devices or other safety safety-critical systems with complex functionality.

Basic elements of root cause using Management Oversight Risk Tree (MORT) Approach Classification

- Materials

  o Defective raw material

  o Wrong type for job

  o Lack of raw material
- Man Power

- o Inadequate capability
- o Lack of Knowledge
- o Lack of skill
- o Stress
- o Improper motivation
- Machine / Equipment
  - o Incorrect tool selection
  - o Poor maintenance or design
  - o Poor equipment or tool placement
  - o Defective equipment or tool
- Environment
  - o Orderly workplace
  - o Job design or layout of work
  - o Surfaces poorly maintained
  - o Physical demands of the task
  - o Forces of nature
- Management
  - o No or poor management involvement
  - o Inattention to task
  - o Task hazards not guarded properly
  - o Other (horseplay, inattention....)
  - o Stress demands
  - o Lack of Process
  - o Lack of Communication
- Methods
  - o No or poor procedures
  - o Practices are not the same as written procedures
  - o Poor communication
- Management system
  - o Training or education lacking

- o Poor employee involvement
- o Poor recognition of hazard
- o Previously identified hazards were not eliminated

BIBLIOGRAPHY

• Aikens, Charlotte A. *Hospital housekeeping*. Detroit Mich: D.T. Sutton, 1910. (162)

• Aikens, Charlotte Albina. *Hospital housekeeping*. Detroit Mich: D.T. Sutton, 1906. (164)

• Bennett S. 1991. Ecopreneuring: The Complete Guide to Small Business Opportunities From the Environmental Revolution. John Wiley and Sons Incorporated. New York.

• Berle, G. 1991. The Green Entrepreneur: Business Opportunities That Can Save the Earth and Make You Money. Liberty Hall Press. New York.

• California Integrated Waste Management Board. 1992. Food For Thought: Restaurant Guide to Waste Reduction and Recycling. California Integrated Waste Management Board. Sacramento, California.

• Carver, Ethel C. *Practical catering: a manual of applied dietetics for schools, institutions and families.*

• Dahl, J. O. *Dictionary of 1001 menu terms, foods, wines, spirits, cocktails.* Stamford Conn: J.O. Dahl, 1936. (47)

• Dahl, J. O. *Dining room management for head waitresses and hostesses.* New York: J. O. Dahl, 1933. (42)

• Earle, Alice Morse. *Stage-coach and tavern days.* New York: Macmillan, 1912. (449)

• Egan, K. 1996. McDonald's Continues Work To Reduce Waste. Waste Age's Recycling Times. May 14: 10.

• Egan, K. 1996. Recycling, Waste Reduction Becoming a Larger Part of the Hotel Industry. Waste Age's Recycling Times. May 14: 13.

• Ferris, D. and C. Shanklin, etal. 1994. Solid Waste Management in Foodservice. Food Technology. March: 110-115.

• Florida Energy Extension Service. 1996. EcoPurchasing for Hotels and Motels (video). University of Florida. Gainesville, Florida.

• Florida Energy Extension Service. 1996. Hotel and Motel Waste Reduction (video). University of Florida. Gainesville, Florida.

• Florida Energy Extension Service. 1996. Recycling in Hotels and Motels (video). University of Florida. Gainesville, Florida.

• Foster, D. 1995. Enthusiasm For Recycling Finally Translates Into Big Business. Las Vegas Review Journal. May 2: 10B.

• Garvin, M. 1992. Alternative Technologies Coming Along. Waste Age. August: 70.

• Grohusko, J. A. *Jack's manual; a treatise on the care and handling of wines and liquors, storing, binning, and serving; recipes for fancy mixed drinks and when and how to serve.* New York: Printed byE. V. Brokaw & bro., 1908. (85)

• Grove, N. 1994. Recycling. National Geographic Magazine. July: 92-115.

• Hamilton, Francis Frazee. *Hotel front desk management, a treatise on the best methods and procedures in use in small hotels.* Miami, Fla.: Francis Frazee Hamilton, 1947. (xvi, 443)

• Hamilton, W. I. *Promoting new hotels: when does it pay?* New York: Harper, 1930. (viii, 158)

• Harding Lawson Associates. 1995. Solid Waste Management Plan For Clark County, Nevada. Clark County Health District. Las Vegas, Nevada.

• Hasek, G. 1991. Hotels Keeping Watch on Waste. Resource Recycling. January: 56-60.

• Hayes, Harriet et al. *College-operated residence halls for women students in 125 colleges and universities.* New York city: Teachers college Columbia university, 1932. (v, 39)

• Hayward, P. 1994. Disney Does Garbage. Lodging. March: 48-58.

- Heinze, Stella E. *The hospital housekeeper's handbook.* Winston-Salem, N C: The Author, 1945. (47 leaves)
- Heinze, Stella E. *The hospital housekeeper's handbook.* Winston-Salem, N C, 1949. (66 l.)
- Hollingsworth, M. 1989. Effect of the Type of Packaging on the Quantity of Solid Waste Generated in Six Selected Food Service Operations. UMI. Ann Arbor, Michigan.
- Hood, J. 1995. How Green Was My Balance Sheet: The Environmental Benefits of Capitalism. Policy Review. Fall: 80-87.
- Hospitality. 1994. Green Globe: HCIMA Backs New Environmental Awareness Initiative. Hospitality. August: 15-17
- Hospitality. 1994. Trinity Road Goes Green. Hospitality. August: 18.
- Jenkins, R. 1993. The Economics of Solid Waste Reduction. Edward Elgar Publishing. Borrkfield, Vermont.
- Jesitus, J. 1993. Pushing the Planet. Hotel and Motel Management. July: 35-36.
- Kharbanda, O. and E. Stallworthy. 1990. Waste Management Towards a Sustainable Society. Auburn House. New York.
- Koenenn, C. 1995. And a Side Order of Recycling. Los Angeles Times. January: E3 Col.1.
- McDowell, E. 1992. Saving by Recycling: The Greening of the Grand Hotel. New York Times. August 8: L37-L41.
- National Park Service, Yosemite Park and Curry Company. 1993. Waste Reduction in Yosemite National Park: An Action Plan. National Park Service.
- National Restaurant Association. 1990. Managing Solid Waste: Answers for the Foodservice Operator. National Restaurant Association. Washington, D.C.
- Nations Restaurant News. 1994. Red Lobster Rolls Recycling Program. Nations Restaurant News. May 6: 30.
- Newell, T. and E. Markstahler. 1993. Commercial Food Waste From Restaurants and Grocery Stores. Resource Recycling. February: 58-61.

- U.S. Environmental Protection Agency. 1993. Waste Prevention Pays Off: Companies Cut Waste in the Workplace. U.S. Environmental Protection Agency. Washington, D.C.

- Wagner, M. 1995. Food Waste Recovery: Just Another Way to Reduce Waste. Resource Recycling. October: 75-77.

- Washington Retail Association. 1992. Preferred Packaging Procurement Guidelines. Washington Retail Association. Olympia, Washington.

- Watkins, E. 1994. Do Guests Want Green Hotels? Lodging Hospitality. April: 70-72.

- Wendehack, Clifford Charles. *Golf & country clubs; a survey of the requirement of planning construction and equipment of the modern club house.* New York: W. Helburn inc., 1929. (li)

- Wendy's Restaurant. 1996. Recycling at Wendy's. Corporate Pamphlet.

- Westerman, M. 1991. Restaurants Recycle. Resource Recycling. January: 78-83.

- Whiffen, H. 1992. Recycling x Energy Savings=Earth's Survival. Florida Hotel and Motel Journal. July: 37.

- White, P. 1983. The Fascinating World of Trash. National Geographic Magazine. April: 425-457.

- Winter, J. and S. Azzimi. 1996. Less Garbage Overnight: A Waste Prevention Guide for the Lodging Industry. ABI Inform. New York.

- Wolff, C. 1994. Living With the Amenity. Lodging Hospitality. April: 65-68.

- Yosemite Concession Services Corporation. 1996. Recycling Program: Yosemite Concession Services. Yosemite Concession Services. Yosemite National Park, California.

- Youde, J. and B. Prenguber. 1991. Classifying the Food Waste Stream. BioCycle. October: 70-71.

- Young Women's Christian Association of the U.S.A. National Board., Jeanette Dutchess, and Emma H.

Index